EVERYBODY'S LYING ABOUT ISLAM

Introduction

On January 27, 2017 Donald Trump signed an executive order "temporarily" banning almost all travel to the United States from seven Muslim countries. The order was poorly implemented, led to great controversy, inspired nationwide protests, and was quickly blocked by the nation's courts.[1] As of this writing, it is largely seen as a defeat for his administration.

But Trump's actions are popular. CNN reports that 47% of Americans support much of his initial executive order.[2] The idea that there is something fundamentally wrong with Islam, and that we need to fight against an entire religion to stay safe is wrong, but it appeals to large audiences in the United States and Europe.

As I will lay out in the essay below, Donald Trump's conception of Islam is deeply flawed. When Trump first proposed a ban on Muslims at the end of 2015, he claimed it would stand, "until we figure out what's going on". If we truly want to do this, and get the United States to deal with what's really going on, we need to acknowledge that Trump is not the only one who is wrong about Islam.

Barack Obama was also wrong about Islam.

So was George W. Bush. In the aftermath of the September 11th attacks, George W. Bush, among many other establishment figures, was quick to insist that there was nothing wrong with Islam. "Islam is a religion of Peace" became the constant refrain. As the essay below will demonstrate, Bush and Obama are closer to the truth than Trump is, but they are not telling the whole story either.

---

[1] http://www.politifact.com/wisconsin/article/2017/feb/03/donald-trumps-executive-order-muslim-ban/

[2] http://www.cnn.com/2017/02/03/politics/donald-trump-travel-ban-poll/

Both sides are presenting partial narratives. The Trumps and Fox news channels of the world want everything to be about the religion. They believe that their uninformed and reductive interpretations of the Koran are enough to condemn 1.6 Billion Muslims worldwide. The establishment types focus on the basic decency and dignity of Islamic people. Some of this comes out of the laudable urge to protect innocents from extremist backlash. But it also stems from geopolitical concerns. This essay will show that combating terrorism has never been Washington DC's primary goal.

Both sides are missing something vital. Organized religions are first and foremost about institutions. It's the institutions that guide people, and tell them how to interpret the ancient and contradictory information that is held in their holy books. And for the past 50 years, Islam's institutions have been corrupted in the most outrageous way.

For half a century, money has been going from the world's gas pumps to Saudi Arabia, and from there to mosques and educational institutions around the world. The Wahabi ideology pushed by the Saudis claims to be the one true Islam, but it isn't, any more than "Prosperity Gospel" American Evangelicalism is the one true Christianity. If a single Christian sect set itself up as the only true way to worship Jesus, there would be a world-wide outcry. But that's exactly what Saudi Arabia has done with its version of Islam, and nobody is making a peep. Almost no one in the United States challenges this narrative, because the issues are complicated, and the academic and journalistic establishments we trust to tell us about the world have been bought off or intimidated. Those in the US who hate Islam are happy to join with Saudi Arabia in claiming that that country's brutal version of the religion is the truth. The United States government has avoided talking about this, because of deep and long-standing connections to Saudi Arabia. The US Establishment narrative has become "Islam is a Religion of Peace" largely in an attempt to deflect attention from its Saudi allies.

This essay will lay out what is really going on with Islam, the United States, and Saudi Arabia. It will explain how the root causes of terrorism have little to do with the fundamental nature of Islam, and everything to do with political choices made in Riyadh and Washington, DC. Riyadh, the capital of Saudi Arabia, has pumped billions of dollars into corrupting Islam worldwide. There is a poison in Islam, but it goes back decades, not centuries. The handful of Muslims that choose to kill for their religion do so for political reasons, not out of "centuries-old" religious ones. "Radical Islamic Terrorism" metastasized due two political events, the war in Afghanistan in the 1980's and today's war in Syria. Washington, DC desperately wants to avoid looking at its role in these events in detail. This essay will do that job. In doing so, it will also illustrate why now may be the best time to revise our long-standing relationship with Saudi Arabia.

Hateful rhetoric on Islam has been gaining strength in the United States. It was one of the forces that led to Donald Trump's election. We need to fight this rhetoric, but we can't really do that until we acknowledge that US establishment obfuscation opened the door.

People think they have been lied to about Islam. They're absolutely right. Everybody's lying about Islam. If we don't start telling the truth then hate will win. We will get exactly the "clash of civilizations" that ISIS wants. We need to start talking about Saudi Arabia. How anybody can talk about radical Islam and terrorism without talking about Saudi Arabia and its 50 years of spreading Islamic extremism is beyond me.

RELIGION

The Koran is an old book, just like the Bible. Both of these books are occasionally ridiculous, barbaric and offensive. If you attempt to take all the prescriptions of these books seriously, you get problems. The perfect Koran inspired society has never existed, just as the perfect Bible inspired society has never existed. People have tried through the centuries, with both books, with differing levels of success.

These books have incredible power. But they're also weirdly neutral. You can use the Bible to uphold a centuries old theocracy. You can also use the bible to overthrow it. In both Islam and Christianity, the holy books have always been used by both revolutionaries and the enforcers of the status quo. Non-religious revolution is kind of a new thing.[3] At any given time these books are being used both to oppress and liberate. In the mid-20th century Roman Catholic liberation theologians in Latin America used the Bible to argue for freedom and dignity, while members of that same Roman Catholic church in Ireland were using the Bible to try to keep Ireland in a pre-modern state.[4] A religious book that claims to show how life should be ordered is a tremendously powerful thing, and it can be used to support any aim you want, from revolution to repression.

People are always trying to mold societies to accord with their visions of these books. The past 500 years of Christianity provide an excellent example. It will be useful to look at this in detail before we get to Islam. In the West we have a number of misconceptions about our own religious history that make it harder to understand what is happening to Islam today.

CHRISTIANITY

---

[3] Or you can argue that it's never gone away. It's possible to see Marxism as a religion too.

[4] http://www.theguardian.com/world/2014/jun/04/claim-of-800-childrens-bodies-buried-at-irish-home-for-unwed-mothers

Throughout medieval Western Europe, the Catholic church's interpretation of the Bible and what it meant held sway. Its insistence on conducting services, and analyzing scripture through the Latin language kept the power of the word of God in their hands. Latin was only available to an educated elite. Power over the Bible was one of the strongest pillars of the Church's power.

With the Reformation, groups all over Europe took this power away, by translating the Bible into local languages, and by imposing their ideas about scripture within individual countries, cities and other areas of political control. Martin Luther had something of a first mover advantage here, and his interpretation dominated large swathes of Germany and Scandinavia for centuries. But once scripture was out from under the centralized Roman church, a bewildering array of sects and interpretations cropped up.

Some went much further than Luther in trying to build biblically inspired communities. Some didn't. The Anglican church, in terms of ritual and organization, preserved much more of Catholic practice than most Protestants, only replacing the Pope with the English king.[5] The Calvinists, as well as a vast array of smaller sects, went much further, running around destroying paintings and sculptures, and imposing a strict version of morality that wouldn't have seemed too alien to the Islamic Fundamentalists of today. Doomsday cults and religious wars proliferated.

In 16th and 17th century Europe, bloody pursuit of your country, town or even family's interpretation of the Bible was common (among a literate

[5] The advisers of Henry VIII's children Edward VI and Elizabeth I tried to push the English Church in a more protestant direction. This all came to a head in the English civil war in the mid 1600s. The fanatics failed. Should you wander in to an Anglican or Episcopal service today, you'll find it to be much more similar to a Catholic one than anything you'd find in a Lutheran or Calvinist church. In the interests of full disclosure, perhaps I should mention that I was raised a member of the Episcopal Church, though I declined confirmation as a teenager. The post US independence Episcopal Church is two "everything Buts" away from Catholicism. Anglicanism was "everything but the Pope", and Episcopalism is the Anglican Church with "everything but the English King".

elite, everybody else got caught up in their battles). It is important to emphasize that then, as now, the majority of people were content to live their lives, and were eager to follow a religious authority they could trust. The "problem" from their perspective was that Reformation era Europe had no single authority to follow. This interacted with politics and the economics of a technologically advancing continent in unpredictable and often horrifying ways. The Thirty Years' War from 1618 to 1648 wiped out a third of the population of the German states, establishing many of our modern ideas about the nation state in the process. It's important to emphasize, that even at its worst, European fanaticism had very strong political and ethnic dimensions as well. The Thirty Years' War, the most cited example of pure religious savagery we have, would not have been possible without very non-spiritual concerns of land and political succession. This is true of today's "religious" conflicts as well.

In the 19th century, massive industrialization provided leisure time and money, inspiring a new wave of religious interest, and a new wave of sects and interpretations. This process continues today. But unlike 20th century Islam, in Europe and the United States economic development and political power were widely dispersed. After the end of the Catholic monopoly it was no longer possible for one interpretation to dominate. Spain, Italy, some German states, and France, to differing degrees, adopted a reformed version of Catholicism[6], but Scandinavia, Great Britain and many German states adopted an array of different interpretations. Eastern Europe was a gloriously heterodox patchwork that the 20th century largely destroyed. Most countries in that region now have a single sect adhered to by the majority of their populations. The United States never had a single approach, and it never will. It's still just possible to describe the countries of Europe and the Americas as "Christian" but there is no chance of ever getting these countries to agree on one version of what precisely Christianity is, or was.[7]

---

[6] The Reformation changed the Catholic Church itself beyond all recognition. The Catholic reform process, dubbed the Counter-Reformation, yielded some spectacularly cheesy religious art, but it also brought sweeping organizational and doctrinal changes that left the institution almost unrecognizable from a Medieval perspective.

[7] Most of my discussion of Christianity is drawn from my own interpretation of the incredible work of Diarmid MacCulloch. He has done an exhaustive survey of the Reformation, as well as a delightful doorstop on the

After hundreds of years of strife, most have agreed to let this go. There are plenty of people who will cheerfully insist that their interpretation of the Christian scriptures is the only valid one, and that anybody who disagrees is certain to burn in hell, but nobody pays attention to those people anymore. Mainstream religious figures throughout the West are generally committed to pleasantly banal concepts like "inter-faith dialogue" and mutual respect. We've moved beyond barely restrained "I guess I won't stab you" toleration, to general good feelings about other people's approaches.

Before we move on to take a look at Islam, and get all snooty about intolerance, it's important to remember that we're not all that far from it in the West. Many were against the idea of a Catholic US president when Kennedy was elected in 1960, and Mitt Romney's Mormonism may have had something to do with the fact that he wasn't elected president in 2012. You don't have to look any further back than World War I to find a religious war in Europe. To be sure there were other more modern and nationalist pathologies that brought that cataclysm about, but the Russian Tsar probably wouldn't have been willing to start the conflagration on behalf of the Serbs if they weren't fellow Eastern Orthodox believers, attacked by the Roman Catholic Austro-Hungarian Empire. Religious conflict came roaring back to Europe in the 1990s. Most know that the Bosnians are Muslims, but few commentators emphasize that the main difference between the Serbs and Croats of the former Yugoslavia is the difference between Eastern Orthodoxy and Roman Catholicism.

ISLAM

50 years ago, Islam was as diverse as Christianity is today. There were religious schools, like the venerable Al-Ahzar university in Cairo, that attempted to establish the correct approach to the Islamic faith, but

---

religion's entire history entitled Christianity: The first 3,000 years. I recommend both highly, especially the history of the whole religion. Having the whole arc of its development in mind is very helpful. Certain themes recur over and over.

diversity was immense. It wasn't just the much-publicized Sunni-Shia divide. There are four schools of thought in mainstream Sunni Islam alone, and there is a galaxy of different sects and approaches both within and completely outside of mainstream Sunni and Shia thought. In a religion stretching from Morocco to the Philippines, it was impossible to impose a single version of doctrine. The generally lower level of development in the Islamic world meant that local interpretations dominated. A pious Islamic leader was unlikely to have the resources to impose one interpretation of Islam on his own dominions, let alone on the hundreds of millions of Muslims present across three continents. Idiosyncratic approaches, including the veneration of local saints and mystic brotherhoods, were found throughout the Islamic world. It was a rich and diverse tradition, far removed from its rigorous sword-spread uniformity of twelve hundred years before.[8] But just like Christianity today, in all this diversity there was somebody working to bring back that old time fire and hate…[9]

THE SAUDS

To understand what has happened to the Islam of today we need to look back, not 50 years, but over 250, to a pact made in the Arabian desert back when most of Europe was still ruled by kings. In 1702 in the village of Najd, the man who would become the cleric Muhammad ibn Abd al-Wahhab was born. After studying in Mecca and Medina, and travelling as far as Basra in modern Iraq, he returned to Najd and began to put his ideas into practice. He wanted to return to the days of the prophet, and cleanse the religion of all aspects that he saw as unfit. As a man who claimed to respect "True Islam" he went about it in an odd way. He smashed the

[8] My general description of Islam draws primarily from two books, Destiny Disrupted: A History of the World Through Islamic Eyes by Tamim Ansary, and No God But God: The Origins, Evolution and Future of Islam by Reza Aslan. I've also done a ton of reading on Islam's political history in the Modern and Pre-Modern era, with too many books to list on the Ottoman empire, and some more limited reading on the history of the 'Stans and Muslim India.

[9] Think that statement is unfair? Then allow me to point you towards the Central African Republic. To be sure, the genocidal inclinations of some African Christians are not on the same scale as the much more publicized efforts of Muslim populations in Nigeria, Somalia and Sudan, but that's because they lack Saudi funds, not because they don't exist. http://www.aljazeera.com/news/2015/07/amnesty-muslims-erased-central-african-republic-150731083248166.html

venerated grave of a companion of the Prophet. He also worked to stamp out pagan remnants such as a grove of sacred trees. Eventually his views became too much for the rulers of Najd and he was expelled.

He found refuge in Diriyah, which was run by the House of Saud. Muhammad bin Saud realized that al-Wahab's uncompromising views were a path to power. The two men formed a pact that has in large part lasted until today. The Sauds agreed to abide by Wahab's unforgiving vision of Islam, and in return the fanaticism mobilized would be used to support the power of the Sauds. The initial vigor of this agreement, established in 1744,[10] allowed their new state to conquer much of the Arabian Peninsula. Within 20 years of Al-Wahab's death in 1791[11] the Saudis managed to take the holy cities of Mecca (1803) and Medina (1805). They had begun to take territory in the old homeland of the Caliphates in Iraq (1802) and Syria (1803) as well.[12] This initial Saudi golden age was short-lived. The Egyptian ruler Muhammad Ali expelled them from the holy cities on behalf of the Ottomans in 1818. The 19th century saw the steady whittling away of Saudi power, until the ruling family was forced to flee to Kuwait in the 1890s.[13]

Their fortunes were restored during the extended collapse of the Ottoman Empire, when the Saudi family, and by extension the Wahabi ideology, received the patronage of the British Empire. This support, and the general level of chaos after World War I, allowed the Sauds to consolidate rule of modern Saudi Arabia by 1932.

Importantly, Ibn Saud, the founder of the modern kingdom, managed to do this through the support of the Ikhwan (The brethren), a fanatical group of Wahabi fundamentalists. This group helped the Sauds take control of Mecca and Medina. They did so with the sorts of massacres and intolerance of other forms of Islam that we see in ISIS related headlines

[10] Gold p. 21
[11] Gold p. 26
[12] Gold p. 21
[13] Gold 17-56. Gold lays out this history at length with only a few errors that I could catch. House is broadly the same, though I initially wrote this piece off of Wikipedia.

today. When elements of the Ikhwan objected to Ibn Saud's coziness with the British, he turned on the fanatics,[14] and defeated them in the battle of Sabilia.[15] This dynamic plays out over and over again in Saudi history. The royal family will occasionally turn on, kill, fire, or try to marginalize certain followers of Wahabi teachings. But at the end of the day the princes need the fanatics, both to maintain control of their fractious kingdom, and to exert influence abroad.

As of 1932, the Sauds had returned, but it didn't mean all that much. They could benefit from pilgrimage to the holy cities, but Saudi Arabia was one of the poorest countries on Earth. Embarrassingly, a good deal of Ibn Saud's ability to run the country in the 1930's came from subsidies from the infidel British.[16] The vast deserts they controlled didn't provide the resources necessary to spread their vehement vision of Islam. They were just a larger version of the semi-colonial Gulf Emirates, weak and unlikely to cause problems for their Western pay-masters.

A Clash Of Civilizations? Or Just In One?

Which brings us back to 50 years ago. As noted above, Islam was as diverse then as Christianity is today. The lower level of development meant that interpretations of scripture were often a good deal more medieval than in modern Christianity, but the diversity was immense. Across Muslim territory, multiple approaches to the problem of development and modernization flourished. To be sure, much of the thinking would strike us in the West as alien, but there was a very real commitment to finding a middle path. Many of the leading thinkers believed that it was possible to find a way to be both Modern and Muslim. The differences between Shia and Sunni interpretations of Islam were much less important than the effort to find a way to meet the challenge that European and American dominance of Muslim lands presented. Those of other religions, even Christians, were often seen as partners in

[14] House Loc. 276
[15] https://en.wikipedia.org/wiki/Ikhwan
[16] Gold p. 59

this effort rather than rivals. The Arab nationalist Ba'ath party, which was to have long and very different careers in Iraq and Syria, emerged in the 1940s, in part out of the ideas of Michel Aflaq, a Christian.

To the extent that there was a "Clash of Civilizations", it was this: It was a clash within Islam to find the appropriate way forward. This clash was inaugurated by Napoleon's rampage through Egypt and Syria from 1798-1801. Though the French eventually left in disgrace, it was the power of the British Navy that kicked them out. The French trounced every land army they came across. This forever dashed comfortable ideas of Islamic superiority for anyone who was looking at the world seriously.

It led to a fascinating range of responses in the Middle East's two most powerful and directly West-facing countries, Egypt and Ottoman Turkey. The Ottoman "Tanzimat" period in the mid 19th century built many of the underpinnings of modern Turkey. It featured oddities like the introduction of religious toleration and equality under the law by an Islamic Caliph. Egypt managed to build itself into a quasi-modern state, that was able to play a convincing game of great power politics. It lost that game equally convincingly by the end of the 19th century. Cosmopolitan intellectuals like Jamāl al-Dīn al-Afghānī, travelled throughout the Muslim world, working carefully to craft a workable blend of Western and Islamic thought.[17] Interestingly, al-Afghānī managed to be both a Pan-Islamist, and the founder and first Grand Master of the Cairo Masonic Lodge.[18]

The Sauds were of course not the only Muslims who reacted with fanaticism. The Mahdi army of Sudan is another famous example. For almost two decades they battled the Egyptian kingdom and the British Empire under a militant version of Islam. This does not mean Islam has some unique pathology. This fanatical retreat to traditional piety is an age-old response to encroaching enemies. It can be seen everywhere, from the falling Eastern Roman empire of the 15th century, to the early 20th century Boxer Rebellion in China, to Russia's rediscovery of the Orthodox church

[17] From the Ruins of Empire: The Revolt Against the West and the Remaking of Asia by Panjak Mishra
[18] https://en.wikipedia.org/wiki/Jam%C4%81l_al-D%C4%ABn_al-Afgh%C4%81n%C4%AB

in our 21st century. Saudi Wahabism, pre-oil, also fits nicely into this framework. The retreat to fanaticism is a common response, and a weak one, that often makes the subjection of the civilization in question more likely rather than less. It is generally through an engagement with the ideas and technology of the newly dominant civilization that a subject people is able to reassert itself.

Unfortunately, the Cold War saw the most powerful leaders in the Muslim world opt for the wrong currents of western thought. US support for Israel forced Arab countries like Syria, Iraq and Egypt[19] further into the Soviet orbit. Militant socialism and strident nationalism dominated. In Egypt and Turkey this led to the expulsion of their ethnic and religious minority commercial classes, and decades of planned economy stagnation. Thug socialism failed over 50 years in Eastern Europe, with a century or so of capitalist development to waste and destroy. Over a similar period it took Syria, Egypt and Turkey from not much to not much more than that. Long before anybody realized how worthless these policies were, something very important happened.

OIL HAPPENS

What happened was Oil. Saudi Arabia was poor as dirt. It was a medieval theocracy poorly suited to any kind of international competition. In fact, this weakness was the reason the country existed. Weakness made it a great partner for both the British Empire and the United States, who have ensured the survival of this odd and pre-modern country for the past century.

Unlike Iran, a country similarly gifted with oil resources, where a vigorous and complex society caused decades of conflict with the United States, followed by an outright break in 1979, the Saudis have been content to keep pumping as long as the checks keep rolling in. Iran nationalized the Anglo-Persian Oil company in 1951, creating the

[19] Egypt was more Soviet for a bit. They made their way back into the US camp by the end of the 1970s under Anwar Sadat.

National Iranian Oil Company (NIOC).[20] This action prompted a US-backed coup in 1953. After the coup, the British were probably disappointed to find that they were incapable of completely reversing the nationalization. They were able get sweetheart deals after the coup, but they couldn't turn back the clock on nationalization. Not even the Shah, an American puppet, could abolish the NIOC and survive. There were too many elements within Iran that would make it impossible. No such problems with the Saudis.

In Saudi Arabia, the US didn't have to deal with the inconveniences of Iran's mobilized populace and vibrant society. The Saudis didn't get around to fully nationalizing Saudi Aramco, their trillion dollar national oil company, until 1980. As long as more money came in, they weren't all that interested in actually controlling the resource. Even today, Saudi Aramco operates as a society within a society, with separate compounds where something like modern life operates, filled with foreigners and the best that Saudi Arabia has to offer.

The weakness of Saudi Arabia was also useful in fending off what used to be the more forward-looking and potentially powerful states of Syria, Egypt and Iraq. These Arab nationalist countries aspired to be modern and secular, and sought legitimacy by portraying themselves as acting in opposition to European, American and Israeli imperialists.[21] This explains the spectacle of a democratic country like the United States allying itself so closely with antiquated monarchies and religious fundamentalism. Saudi Arabia and the other Gulf emirates may be against everything we stand for, and terrible for their people, but they're weak and outmoded enough to have no choice but to sell us their oil.[22]

The alien nature of Saudi society and culture wasn't a problem for the relationship with the US. In fact, it made it stronger. The Saudis knew that in order to continue to run their affairs unmolested, they had to provide

---

[20] https://cdn.loc.gov/master/frd/frdcstdy/ir/irancountrystudy00curt_0/irancountrystudy00curt_0_djvu.txt

[21] Davidson

[22] Davidson is very strong on this.

services that no other country would provide. And that's exactly what they did. They cycled their money back into the US economy, and they were very careful to help out whenever the CIA or some other element of the US military industrial complex came calling. Perhaps most importantly, they were willing to open their check books for billions of dollars worth of US and European military technology. This close relationship with defense contractors has guaranteed that their actions receive only token scrutiny from Washington, DC, London and Brussels.

This cooperation shaped the history of the 20th century, in the Middle East and beyond. The Saudis helped to fund the Reagan administration's dirty wars in Latin America and Africa. After Iran booted the Shah in the 1979 revolution, the Saudis spent 10s of billions of dollars on Saddam Hussein's war against Iran. The US fully supported Saudi Arabia's creation of Iraq's military machine. The Iran-Iraq war included vicious trench warfare and the use of chemical weapons against both soldiers and civilians. Taking place throughout the 1980s it provided a horrific 70-year late flashback to World War I. It may have killed as many as a million people, and it has a lot to do with how screwed up the Iranian regime is today. We wouldn't have been able to do it without the Saudis.

The Saudi role in devastating Iran and Iraq is obvious, but what they've managed to do to Islam as a whole is much more significant. Saudis have paid for Madrassahs and severe Koranic literalism throughout the world. Countries like Afghanistan and Pakistan were completely transformed by this influence, but Islamic practice in every country has been warped by Saudi money.

The most obvious result of this process was 9/11. Yes, Saudi Arabia was both indirectly and, to some degree, directly responsible for 9/11, but they weren't the only ones. We'll get to that in more detail later. Saudi Arabia should be held to account for that. It's not exactly breaking new ground to mention this. What hasn't been mentioned as much, however, is a very different crime that Saudi Arabia has committed. It's not as flashy as terrorism, but I think it's much worse. For the past 50 years the Saudis have been carrying out a sort of cultural genocide against religious diversity within Islam itself.

WHAT THE SAUDIS DID TO ISLAM

For 400 years the Malian Empire dominated a stretch of Northwest Africa. Its rulers were extraordinarily wealthy. In 1324 one of them set off runaway inflation in Egypt just by traveling through on a pilgrimage to Mecca.[23] One legacy of this empire is the extraordinary libraries of Timbuktu. They contain manuscripts, dating back to the 14th century, covering the full range of Islamic culture, history and science. Few of the volumes have been adequately preserved and digitized, making these libraries a largely un-discovered resource for scholarship. Though the modern country of Mali has been impoverished for quite some time, private libraries consisting of thousands of volumes still exist throughout Timbuktu.[24] Many are in private houses, but there are also larger institutions that preserve this extraordinary cultural resource.

One such institution was the Ahmed Baba Institute in Sankore. On January 25, 2013 Saudi-inspired Islamic fundamentalists burned it to the ground.[25] The foresight and daring of Malian librarians managed to save the majority of the institute's 20,000 volumes, but as many as 4,000 manuscripts, some dating back 600 years, were lost.[26] Thanks to those valiant librarians, the bulk of Timbuktu's manuscripts were saved from the city's brief radical Islamist government (March 2012- February 2013).

Please note that most of our librarian-heroes were Muslim as well.

It is not Islam that's the problem, it is Saudi Arabian Islam. Timbuktu was taken over by a combination of Al Queda in the Islamic Maghreb, and Ansar Dine, the Taureg Islamic fundamentalist group that took a number of Northern Malian cities in 2012,[27] prompting French intervention. Iyad

---

[23] "Mansa Musa and Islam in Africa: Crash Course World History #16 https://www.youtube.com/watch?v=jvnU0v6hcUo
[24] https://en.wikipedia.org/wiki/Timbuktu_Manuscripts
[25] https://www.theguardian.com/world/gallery/2013/jan/28/ahmed-baba-library-torched-islamist-pictures
[26] https://mentalfloss.atavist.com/the-great-library-rescue-of-timbuktu
[27] https://en.wikipedia.org/wiki/Operation_Serval#/media/File:Northern_Mali_conflict.svg

Ag Ghaly, the founder of Ansar Dine, was once a more run of the mill African revolutionary, running an outfit called the Popular Movement for the Liberation of Azawad in the 1990s. It was his three-year period (2005-2008) in Saudi Arabia that turned him into a book burner. He reportedly experienced a "religious re-birth" and made the contacts necessary to make his 2012 insurgency possible.[28]

A more famous example of Saudi inspired cultural vandalism happened in the Bamiyan province of Afghanistan in 1997. Two 1,500 year old statues of the Buddha, one of which stood 170 feet high, were destroyed by the Taliban. This is horrific of course, but the crime in Mali strikes me as worse. It is a crime against a living community. Buddhism died out in Afghanistan almost 1,000 years ago. Rather than some antique remnant, the fundamentalists in Mali are attempting to extinguish a living tradition. They don't just want to kill other forms of Islam, they want to make it as if other forms of Islam never existed.

Saudi cultural imperialism happened on an extreme level in Afghanistan. All the worst elements of Saudi ideology were given free reign. But the Afghani Taliban is only the most obvious example of how Saudi influence has managed to be so powerful throughout the world. Oil riches have rocketed Saudi Arabia into a category of economic development far beyond most of their co-religionists. Despite the country's lack of many of the hallmarks of modern civilization, many Saudi Arabians lead a distinctly first world lifestyle. The places where their proselytizing has had the most success, like Africa and some of the 'Stans, are desperately poor. More Muslim countries are catching up economically, but throughout the 20th century it was hard for any local Islamic authorities to compete with folks who speak Arabic[29], control Mecca and Medina, and own the jet they came to meet you and your donkey with.

[28] https://en.wikipedia.org/wiki/Iyad_Ag_Ghaly

[29] Arabic is the holy language of Islam. The koran is translated into other languages, but all concede that the Arabic version is the only divine one.

Saudi Power didn't just provide influence over the very poor. Egypt, the previous intellectual leader of the Arab World, was susceptible as well. Under Anwar Sadat in the 1970s Egypt migrated to the US camp from the Soviet camp. Saudi money played a role in this as well. As part of the switch, the 1,000 year old Al-Azhar university stepped up its relationship with Saudi clerics. This made the Egyptian university, the most prestigious in Sunni Islam,[30] much richer, and much more conservative.[31] Signing Sunni spiritual and political leadership over to the faux-developed country of Saudi Arabia, from the semi-developed country of Egypt has had a devastating effect on world Islam. Much of this effect is outside of the scope of this essay, but I'm confident there are at least a dozen great dissertations there.

It's as if John Calvin and his biblical literalists found a mountain of silver or something in the 1500s. Thankfully they didn't, and religious diversity was able to survive and inoculate European civilization against the Bible's worst excesses. Islam has not been so lucky. It's exactly this economic imbalance between the oil-rich and the rest of the Islamic countries that has made Saudi Arabia's influence so pernicious and so widespread.

To truly understand what Saudi Arabia has done to Islam, first we have to look at what Saudi Arabia has done to itself.

What Saudi Arabia Has Done To Itself

That deal made between Wahab and the first Saudi king all the way back in the 18th century still holds today. The Wahabi religious authorities, known as the Ulema, guide the religion of the country and provide the legitimacy that holds the countries estimated 90-odd tribes together. The King protects the religion, and is able to guide and profit from the state that does that. The deal has lasted for centuries but that doesn't mean it is

[30] https://en.wikipedia.org/wiki/Al-Azhar_University
[31] Davidson p. 20

a stable one.[32] It provides the weakness that made Saudi Arabia so attractive to the British Empire and the United States. A successful and well established king like Ibn Saud, who guided modern Saudi Arabia's founding, can push back against religious elements like the Ikhwan. Weaker kings, or kings that need permission to do things that the Ulema doesn't like have to trade things for that ability.

"Needing permission to do things the Ulema doesn't like" describes every single Saudi king since Ibn Saud. Wahabi teachings are fanatically anti-everybody that isn't Wahabi. Anyone who doesn't agree with their interpretation of Islam is to be converted, exterminated or subjugated. This obviously includes everyone from the West, be they Christian, or even worse non-believers or Jews. Since the time of Ibn Saud, and the beginning of the oil industry, Western involvement has been steadily escalating. The exploitation of these resources requires a lot of infidel penetration into Saudi Arabia, which is supposed to be the Wahabi Ulema's special realm of perfect Islam. The Ulema hates that obviously. It also brings a ton of money though, which the Ulema enjoys very much. So as Saudi Arabia has gotten richer, its rulers have had to devote more and more funds to placating the religious establishment. This is an extremely delicate balance. King Saud, Ibn Saud's first successor failed to do it correctly, and the Ulema deposed him in 1964.[33] All Saudi Kings are presumably quite conscious of this abbreviated reign, and are careful to get that balance right.

When King Faisal took over in 1964 he knew he had to incorporate the Ulema in his government.
Thanks to oil money there was a lot more government to go around, with 14 new ministries added between 1960 and 1975, bringing the total to 23. The Saud family held on to foreign affairs, finance and defense, the only three ministries that dated back to before 1951, but the Ulema penetrated deeply into the rest. They controlled the ministry of Justice, and most

[32] Both House and Gold deal with this tension on almost every page of their respective books. Davidson covers it as well.

[33] Gold p. 125 https://en.wikipedia.org/wiki/King_of_Saudi_Arabia

importantly the Ulema has controlled the Ministry of Education since Faisal's accession in 1964.[34] By 2000, a country that had had negligible educational infrastructure thirty years before now had a growing primary, secondary and university system. But it was a different kind of university from what we're used to in the west. As Dore Gold puts it:

> In 1965 there were 3,625 university students throughout the Saudi Kingdom; by 1986 the number had reached 113,529.... Thirty percent of Saudi students in Saudi universities majored in Islamic studies, while the other 70 percent devoted an average of a third of their coursework to religious study.[35]

It should go without saying that all of this religious study was Wahabi.

1979: It Gets Worse

In 1979 the balancing act facing the Saudi kings got even more difficult. The replacement of the pro-American and Saudi-Friendly Shah of Iran by a revolutionary Shia government made the neighborhood much more dangerous. The Iran-Iraq war that Saudi Arabia largely paid for created a hyper-militarized monster to the north in the form of Saddam Hussein. During the 1980s, oil shipments needed to be protected from the Iranian air force and navy, and during the 1990s the entire country needed to be protected from the Iraqi military machine the Saudis had helped to build. All of this meant US military protection, offshore in the Persian Gulf in the 1980s, and in the country itself in the 1990s. Obviously the Ulema hated all of this.

Adding to the complications, a bunch of young Saudis, with interesting connections to high levels of the Ulema,[36] decided to violently protest all this Western involvement. On November 20th, 1979 the extremists seized the Grand Mosque in Mecca, Islam's holiest site. It took two weeks and

[34] Gold ps 77-78
[35] Gold p. 79
[36] Gold p. 106

cost at least 1,000 lives to get them out. This required the use of French commandos, further highlighting the Saudi government's inadequacies.[37]

The extremists were killed but they won. The Saudi government reacted with an intensification of their commitment to Wahabi principles, involving new repression of women, the exorcising of as many western influences as was practicable, and a newly energized religious police force enforcing all of it.[38] This yielded an incredible paradox. As Saudi Arabia got closer to the United States, both involuntarily in the waters of the Persian Gulf, and voluntarily in Soviet occupied Afghanistan, its development and promotion of a fervently anti-Western ideology also accelerated.

Honestly, reviewing all of this, it's almost possible to build some sympathy for the Saudi Kings. They have built a trap for themselves that gets steadily more and more complicated. It'd be easier to be sympathetic if it weren't for those private jets with hot tubs.

The balancing act was somewhat eased by rising oil revenues from the 1930s through the 1970's. It didn't stop in the 1970's, in fact it got exponential. The initial OPEC oil shock in 1973 sent prices into the stratosphere. The steady disruption of Iranian production after 1979 kept them up there. Prices came back to Earth in the late 1980s and 1990s, but then China's rise got them going again. From the 1970s until 2014 Saudi Arabia's rulers had an ever-growing pool of toys to play with. They used those toys to try to destroy world-wide Islam.

What The Saudis Did To Everybody Else

Saudi Arabia has 28 million people. A surprisingly large number of them are desperately poor.[39] But almost every level of this society from princes to paupers has been engaged in a world-wide project of Islamic

[37] House loc. 321, Gold pps. 106-111, Davidson p. 112
[38] House loc. 1300
[39] House

extremism. If it were just the government it would be fairly straightforward to shut this process down, but it's not, and we haven't even done that. The Saudi royal family is now counted in the tens of thousands. Many of these people are fabulously wealthy, some are merely well-off by western standards.[40] Beyond the royals there is a significant upper class of families like the Bin Ladens who have also become fabulously wealthy. All Muslims have the duty of Zakat, one of the five pillars of Islam, requiring almsgiving for religious purposes. In Saudi Arabia the "religious purpose" is often the spread of the Wahabi creed.

The network of Saudi charities that exists to take this money has been doing the work of destroying Islam. Some of these organizations are outright funders of terror, but most are not. Instead they build mosques, and fund educational systems that push an extremist version of Islam that stops just short of suggesting violence.
This is an important point. Radicalization is a cumulative process. People don't just wake up one day thinking: "I'm going to go out and kill somebody for my religion". People need to be convinced of a number of other things first. A lot needs to go into an ideology that convinces a person to murder innocents.

Most terrorism in the 21st century is carried out by radical Sunni Muslims. Some credit Iran-inspired Shia radicals for inventing the modern practice of suicide bombing, but I can't think of a high-profile example after the 1990s. Others credit the Tamil Tigers of Sri Lanka, who were Hindu to some degree, but that civil war is over. All the big recent stuff is an offshoot of Sunni Islam, and the specific Saudi Wahabi interpretation. 9/11, Al Queda, ISIS, Al-Shabab, Boko Haram, etc. etc. etc., it's all Sunni.

So let's take a look at what a Sunni Radical has to believe to go out and kill people.

1. The Koran is more important than Democracy

[40] That House thing about just making 19 grand a month.

2. Most interpretations of the Koran from the past 1000 years aren't just wrong they are evil.
3. Modern life is useless and evil.
4. Infidels are bad and sub-human.
5. OK, let's go out and kill people!

All five of these steps have been encouraged by Saudi-funded mosques throughout the world. Since Al Queda took its war to Saudi Arabia in 2004 and 2005, the Saudi establishment has really backed off on pushing step 5 in this process. A number of Saudi radicals were jailed and executed, and Saudi clerics that celebrated 9/11 and violent jihad against the West were silenced in one way or another. But that's it. Steps one through four are still very much a part of the world-wide teachings of Saudi charities.

Rudy Giuliani, the high profile former mayor of New York, insists that Saudi Arabia is now a new and different country because of this small change.[41] I think that's bonkers. According to Rudy and others, Saudi Arabia is a "valued partner" in the perpetual motion machine of what used to be called the "War on Terror". The Saudis are now eager to participate with Western intelligence services in the pursuit of those who step over the line into terrorist activities against the West and the Saudi regime. But Saudi "charities" still pour billions of dollars into bringing people up to that line.

And the funding for step 5, "Let's go out and kill people!", has only dried up with respect to Saudi Arabia and the West, and only from official channels. Violent Sunni fundamentalist organizations are still supported by the Saudi government across the Middle East and North Africa. Private funding still makes Saudi Arabia a hub of funding for the "really bad" Jihadist groups like ISIS. As the Guardian ably documented in 2010, private sources in Saudi Arabia are still the largest source of funds for Al-Queda and a range of jihadist organizations throughout India and Africa.[42]

---

[41] https://www.youtube.com/watch?v=JTYjBwo5Uig

[42] https://www.theguardian.com/world/2010/dec/05/wikileaks-cables-saudi-terrorist-funding

Much of this "charitable" work happens independently, and no serious effort has been made to control the amounts involved. But the Saudi Government itself has put an extraordinary amount of money into spreading Wahabism. The umbrella organizations through which much of these funds are distributed are the Muslim World League(MWL), founded in 1962, and the International Islamic Relief Organization (IIRO), founded in 1978. Details of how these organizations work are maddeningly difficult to find, but nobody disputes that they are primarily concerned with funding and supporting Wahabi Islam.

The character of the work of these organizations is capably demonstrated in a New York Times article from 2015.[43] In 2015 the Saudi state organized a conference in Mecca entitled "Islam and Countering Terrorism". Meant to counter the rise of ISIS, it arrived at the ludicrous conclusion that what was needed to combat ISIS was a more rigorous form of Islam and the promotion of Sharia law world-wide. In a rarity for the New York Times, the writer explicitly called out the hypocrisy of the Saudi State and its "...decades long role in aggressively spreading its strictly conservative religious ideology – a creed that itself has provided inspiration for the leaders of the Islamic State..."[44]

This spread has indeed been aggressive. A comprehensive report from U.S. News & World Report claimed that between 1975 and 2002 the Saudis spent **70 billion dollars** on international aid, and that two thirds of that aid was spent on promoting Wahabi Islam.[45] The spending has not slowed down since. It accelerated throughout the oil boom that ended in 2014. Some estimate that Saudi Arabia still dedicates two to three billion dollars every year to spreading Wahabi thought internationally.[46] The

[43] https://www.nytimes.com/2015/03/19/world/middleeast/islamic-scholars-promote-sharia-as-an-alternative-to-extremism.html

[44] https://www.nytimes.com/2015/03/19/world/middleeast/islamic-scholars-promote-sharia-as-an-alternative-to-extremism.html

[45] This article is devilishly difficult to find. It's not available on-line, and it's not available on Pro-Quest. I'm reduced to quotes of the article on other pages. http://www.historycommons.org/entity.jsp?entity=muslim_world_league

[46] http://www.independent.co.uk/news/uk/home-news/wahhabism-a-deadly-scripture-398516.html

extent to which the other third of those 70 billion dollars can be separated out from the promotion of radical ideology is debatable. When Saudi Arabia builds a mosque somewhere, it naturally has a say in the version of Islam that is promoted in that mosque.

Consider that 70 billion USD figure again. A significant share of this spending has been directed to places like Africa, Afghanistan, and the post-Soviet 'stans. That amount of money would go pretty far anywhere. In under developed countries it has the capability to change everything, and it has.

Direct links between these organizations and terrorism are not hard to find. The IIRO employed Osama Bin Laden's brother in law in the Phillipines and Indonesia.[47] They also employed the brother of Ayman Al-Zawahiri, the current head of Al-Queda, in Albania.[48] These direct links have, of course, been cleaned up since 9/11, but I'd argue that they aren't the most troubling aspect of the work of these organizations anyway.

What matters is the ideology. These organizations have fundamentally changed the practice of Islam, and introduced concepts and approaches that are alien to centuries of local tradition. The pattern repeats in country after country.

A Wahabi World Tour

What follows is a not at all comprehensive tour of the way Wahabi ideas have influenced a selection of countries I am familiar with.

Let's start in North Africa…

Morocco has been able to avoid destabilization by Wahabi Islamists. This was not just luck. Despite close relations with Saudi Arabia, a fellow Arab

[47] https://en.wikipedia.org/wiki/International_Islamic_Relief_Organization#Albania
[48] Gold 243

Monarchy, the Moroccan government felt it necessary to put a program in place to counter Wahabi ideas.[49] The country's "Islamic Reform" program was started in 2003 after suicide bombings in Casablanca. Over the years, the state has trained 100,000 Imams in North Africa's traditional Maliki school of Sunni Islam.[50] This program has also involved the suppression of independent preachers of intolerance.[51] State support and control of religion is something that my Western upbringing prompts me to dislike. But for Islamic countries fending off the Wahabi onslaught it is an essential survival strategy.

Morocco's tourism receipts and competently run economy have allowed them to do this. The rest of Muslim North West Africa isn't so lucky.

In Mali, as documented above, Saudi money funds extreme political instability and the destruction of the country's Islamic heritage.

In Northern Nigeria, Boko Haram makes international headlines with its savagery. Whole villages are wiped out in single attacks. 70% of Northern Nigeria lives on less than a dollar a day, but Boko Haram seems to have limitless resources.[52] Many cling to the idea that Boko Haram somehow buys its armored vehicles and AK-47s by exploiting local black markets. This is another strategy used to avoid the reality of Gulf state funding. Just as with Mali, Boko Haram's path to wealth and extremism lies through Saudi Arabia.

Boko Haram was founded in 2002 by Mohammed Yusuf, who studied at the University of Medina in Saudi Arabia.[53] The Washington Post reports that when Nigeria first cracked down on the organization, Yusuf fled to Saudi Arabia, where he found new contacts with Al Queda, and more

---

[49] https://divinity.uchicago.edu/sightings/moroccos-program-securing-religious-toleration-model-region
[50] http://nypost.com/2015/08/13/fighting-terror-bogart-style-how-morocco-counters-radical-islam/
[51] https://divinity.uchicago.edu/sightings/moroccos-program-securing-religious-toleration-model-region
[52] https://www.washingtonpost.com/news/morning-mix/wp/2014/06/06/this-is-how-boko-haram-funds-its-evil/?utm_term=.7b54776f3606
[53] https://en.wikipedia.org/wiki/Mohammed_Yusuf_(Boko_Haram)

funding.[54] Despite the Nigerian government's repeated declarations of victory, the north remains a battle ground, with Boko Haram pledging allegiance to ISIS in 2015.[55]

Algeria's military dictatorship has worked hard to suppress radical Islamists, fighting a murderous civil war against them from 1991-2002. The war killed as many as 150,000 people. Many of the most dangerous opposition fighters were veterans of the US-Saudi war in Afghanistan. They brought Saudi Wahabism back with them.

Tunisia is seen as the most westernized of Arab countries. The stability of one of Africa's more enlightened dictatorships, under Bourguiba from 1956 to 1987 and Ben Ali from 1987 to 2011, joined with a healthy tourism industry and a commitment to secularism served the country well. Tunisia remains the Arab Spring's sole success story, maintaining a troubled but functioning system of representative government six years later. This success story also included firm control of religion. Under the dictatorship, all mosques were owned and controlled by the government. The new more democratic form of government continues to struggle against imported radicalism. The balance between freedom of speech and the fight against radicalization has been difficult to maintain. Tunisia has been the largest contributor of foreign fighters to the Jihad against Assad in Syria.[56]

Libya under Gaddafi's absolutist system was subject to his idiosyncratic views of Islam rather than Saudi Arabia's.[57] NATO's destruction of his regime in 2011 has created a new opening for Wahabi thought. Though ISIS seems to have lost ground in Libya in 2016,[58] Saudi Arabia and the Gulf countries continue to fund multiple groups of radical Islamist militias that make the country ungovernable as of this writing.

---

[54] https://www.washingtonpost.com/news/morning-mix/wp/2014/06/06/this-is-how-boko-haram-funds-its-evil/?utm_term=.7b54776f3606
[55] https://en.wikipedia.org/wiki/Boko_Haram#History
[56] https://en.wikipedia.org/wiki/Islam_in_Tunisia
[57] https://en.wikipedia.org/wiki/Islam_in_Libya
[58] http://www.cnn.com/2016/09/16/middleeast/sirte-libya-final-stand-isis/

The unfolding disaster in Syria and Iraq will be covered below.

Saudi influence is not limited to the Middle East.

Doing justice to Wahabi influence in Pakistan and India would fill a book. Pakistan's continued destabilization by Saudi inspired Jihadi elements is a familiar story to anybody who follows the news. India and Pakistan remain the two countries most likely to get into a nuclear war. Should that doomsday scenario ever come about, it is likely that Saudi influenced militants will play a leading role.

Russia has more to lose to Wahabization than is widely recognized. One of the more popular conspiracy theories about the Syrian Civil War is that it was all part of a Russian master plan. They wanted Sunni radicalization and massive refugee flows because of its potential to end the European Union. This is bonkers. Syria is a nightmare for Russia, both because of the weakening of one of its few allies, and a simple demographic fact we all like to ignore. Germany is 5% Muslim. France is 7% Muslim. Russia is at least 14% Muslim and is already losing control over parts of its territory to Sunni radicalization. Chechnya is nominally back under Russian control at the moment, but you only have to look at the beard and the Instagram feed of its leader Ramzan Kadyrov to realize that the country is falling out of Russia's European orbit. This radicalization dates back to the Cold War, and a US-Saudi program of sponsoring Islamic fundamentalism in the USSR.

The threat of organized ISIS attacks that never really materializes in the United States is a daily reality in Russia.[59] Russia obviously didn't want the war in Syria to start, but now that it has they certainly fear its end. Islamic radicalism is already spreading from Chechnya to other Russian provinces like Tatarstan and Bashkortostan.[60] Many of the most fearsome fighters on the Iraqi and Syrian battle field are Russian speakers. The most

[59] https://warontherocks.com/2016/12/the-coming-of-the-russian-jihad-part-ii/
[60] https://warontherocks.com/2016/12/the-coming-of-the-russian-jihad-part-ii/

likely victim of a post-Syria, Algeria-style "returning Jihadist" civil war is Russia.

Since the 1970s Muslim majority Malaysia has seen a swing towards conservatism. As pointed out below, some of this can be credited to the natural swing towards religious conservatism that comes with economic development. But few doubt that Islam's development in Malaysia has been seriously impacted by Saudi Arabia. In the 1970s few Malaysian women used the traditionally rural "Tudong" head covering. Now the majority of Muslim women do.[61]

From the 1970s Saudi Arabia has been massively involved with Malaysia's religious development. They funded the establishment of the International Islamic University of Malaysia, and they have been a large contributor towards the Muslim Welfare Organization of Malaysia. Saudi Arabia operates a Malay language radio station, and has been pumping Wahabi religious materials into the country for decades.[62]

Malaysia's economic miracle over the past decades has made the relationship more balanced, but Saudi intolerance has laid deep roots in the country. To distract from corruption problems, the ruling party is now weighing the introduction of Sharia law inspired punishments. This effort failed in 2016, but it remains an issue. The Muslim majority is becoming less and less tolerant of the 37% of Malaysia that practices other religions.[63] Traditional, more heterodox Islamic practices are being stamped out in favor of Sunni orthodoxy. The degree to which Malaysia's transformation can be credited to Saudi Arabia is beyond my knowledge of the country. But it is undeniable that Wahabi thought has had an impact.

Indonesia, the world's largest Muslim majority country has done a better job managing Saudi influence. Despite being 87% Muslim, the country

[61] https://en.wikipedia.org/wiki/Islam_in_Malaysia
[62] http://www.mei.edu/content/malaysia-saudi-arabia-relations-roots-dimensions-and-prospects
[63] http://www.economist.com/news/leaders/21707537-malaysias-government-stirring-up-religious-tensions-distract-attention-its-own

has no ethnic majority, with the largest group, the Javanese barely cresting 40% of the population. The country's government was radically decentralized with the advent of democracy in the late 1990s.[64] Indonesia is made up of multiple islands, and some areas are majority non-Muslim. Wahabi style Muslim supremacy isn't consistent with holding the country's diverse lands and peoples together. The country's size and complexity also means that older, more local practices of Islam have done a better job of surviving the Saudi onslaught.

Aceh, Indonesia's westernmost province has changed the most. Since 2001 this 98% Muslim province has been governed under a version of Sharia law.[65] The code does not include mutilation but it does include flogging for certain offenses. This is controversial, both within Indonesia and abroad. It has a lot of support within the province however. The evolution of Sharia in Aceh should be watched closely, but it is worth emphasizing that it is a local solution. I'm of the opinion that democracy is a good thing, even when it produces results that are troubling to my Western eyes. If a people wants a certain system, it's better that it be tried out than crushed. Democracy is better than insurgency, and its effects in Aceh have been positive. Burma, Thailand and the Philippines are all dealing with decades long Islamic insurgencies that have killed thousands. Indonesia used to have one of those too. Aceh's insurgency petered out in 2005, four years after the introduction of local control of religious affairs.

Nonetheless, it's important to note that Wahabi style politics are becoming more important in Indonesia. The incumbent governor of Jakarta, known as Ahok, is a Chinese Christian. Jakarta is both Indonesia's most populous city, and the capital of the country. In the run up to the first round of elections in February 2017, large numbers of Muslims protested Ahok's candidacy on the grounds that he is a Christian. Tens of thousands of people participated.[66] Ahok managed to win the first

---

[64] http://www.worldpolicy.org/blog/2014/03/12/why-democracy-does-not-come-easily-indonesia

[65] https://www.nytimes.com/2017/01/12/world/asia/indonesia-sharia-law-aceh.html?_r=0

[66] http://www.economist.com/news/asia/21717095-ahok-embattled-chinese-christian-tops-vote-governor-jakarta-half-victory

round of voting on February 15th, but it remains to be seen whether he can win the second round of elections in April. The Saudi connection here is of course not mentioned much, but it's easy to find. Where do you think Muhammad Rizieq Shihab, the leader of the anti-Ahok movement, was educated? This self-proclaimed leader of Indonesia's Muslims[67] received his degree in Islamic jurisprudence and education from King Saud University in Riyadh, Saudi Arabia.

The success of Wahabi thought in Europe is hard to explain. Shouldn't some of the most developed countries on Earth be able to shield their countries from foreign ideologies? Apparently not. Handfuls of European Muslims have been radicalized, and not just the poor ones. Some of them have included fairly high level professionals. This is harder to puzzle, but I'd imagine it mostly comes down to alienation. There is a tremendous disconnect between the world that Saudi ideology depicts and the world as it is. And no matter the individual success of certain individuals in Europe's Muslim diaspora, the European Muslim community doesn't have the resources necessary to guide its own religion. Far more European Muslims are in the slums on the outskirts of Paris and other cities than in professional schools. These people at the bottom of the European economic distribution probably give what they can to their local mosque, but it isn't much.

As bizarre as it may seem, Gulf money is as important for Islam in Europe as it is for Islam in Africa. Much of European Christianity remains state supported to some degree. Established churches benefit from tax money in countries as diverse as Germany, Austria, Italy, Denmark, and Finland.[68] Christian churches in Europe that do not benefit from direct government funding have centuries of endowments, tradition, and significant charitable giving to draw upon. European Mosques have none of this. They have largely been built and shaped by money from Saudi Arabia and other Wahabi sympathizing Gulf States.

---

[67] http://www.economist.com/news/asia/21717095-ahok-embattled-chinese-christian-tops-vote-governor-jakarta-half-victory

[68] https://en.wikipedia.org/wiki/Church_tax

Much has been made of the fact that larger fractions of European Muslims are sympathetic to the actions of some terrorists.[69] To my mind, these figures are actually quite heartening. The scariest of these polls, carried out with dubious methodology, by right wing outlets, rarely find that more than 10-20% of European Muslims are sympathetic to organizations like ISIS.[70] Considering what you know now about the source of most Islamic ideology in Europe, isn't that impressive? Further, these polls often show that support for these organizations is concentrated among the young and angry.

The basic truth remains that the vast majority of Muslims across the world are decent, peaceful people. The fact that they've remained so in the face of half a century of Saudi propaganda is quite extraordinary.

In 2015 France woke up to the fact that their neglect of Islam has allowed it to be shaped by the religion's worst elements internationally.[71] Efforts to stamp out funding by Qatar and Saudi Arabia continue, but in order to do so legally other sources of revenue must be found.[72] Once they are, however, the question of "European Islamic Radicalism" should be relatively easy to solve.

Other countries, such as Austria, have taken action to get foreign funding out of their mosques[73]. This is of course problematic. As a proud US citizen, I'm a big fan of freedom of religion, widely defined. But I would argue that these measures against Gulf influence are necessary. As we saw with our brief survey above, the countries that have done best against the Wahabi onslaught are those who have taken proactive steps to police the practice of Islam in their own countries. Full control of religion is of course impossible in the context of European human rights. That's a good thing. But taking the step to cut out foreign influence and funding is both

[69] http://www.thereligionofpeace.com/pages/articles/opinion-polls.aspx
[70] https://policyexchange.org.uk/
[71] http://en.rfi.fr/general/20150215-france-cut-qatar-funding-mosques-crackdown-islamic-fundamentalism
[72] http://www.thelocal.fr/20160314/french-politician-calls-for-halal-tax-to-fund-mosque-building
[73] https://www.theguardian.com/world/2015/mar/08/austria-foreign-minister-islam-funding-law-restricting

necessary and proper. Islam in Europe will then be free to take its own path.

It's tragic when European Muslims, some of the people best situated to form a new fusion between Islam and modernity, are led astray by Jihadi dreams. It's important to remember though, that the people we're talking about here are only slightly more prevalent than mass shooters in the United States. And that's only if you include all the young men and women who are drawn to join the various groups fighting in Syria. Without the political encouragement of the Syrian conflict, even fewer Muslim Europeans would have made the full jump to radicalization.

The European failure to integrate its Muslim population is highlighted by US success. The 3.3 million Muslims in the United States have not fallen for Saudi radicalism in any significant way. This is despite the fact that there is a good deal of Saudi money sloshing around Islamic institutions in the United States. My country provides a well-worn framework for assimilation, and greater economic opportunity. To be sure, there have been attacks by homegrown radicals. But attacks like San Bernardino and Orlando stem more from a very American culture of mass shooting than from the coordinated networks we see in Europe.

Interestingly, the Saudi influence is stronger among those who hate Islam in the United States than among those who love it. Because the US establishment has no interest in challenging worldwide Wahabism, and often acts to encourage it, the Saudi interpretation of Islam is accepted as the model. When I argue with US Islamophobes online, I am often struck by how limited their base of knowledge is. My discussion partner can tell me about Saudi rules on Apostasy, and the number of public executions that take place in the country each year. When he talks about "Sharia Law" he is almost exclusively talking about Saudi Sharia law, with its pile of severed heads and limbs. This particularly fierce interpretation of Islamic law can only be found in Saudi Arabia, and in the few African and Afghan regions that were poor enough to have it imposed by Saudi educated clerics. Iran, with its extreme theocratic government, also engages in these punishments. Online Islamophobes typically know nothing of India, Indonesia, Malaysia, and other large countries where the majority of the world's Muslims actually live. Though many of these countries incorporate Sharia law to some degree, none of them feature any amputations or executions. An attempt to introduce a few of these punishments democratically failed in Muslim majority Malaysia in 2016.[74]

It's incredible how successful this international program of Wahabi propaganda has been. It has long been recognized by lone academics and journalists as a problem.[75] Yet progress is slow, and public awareness of these issues is low. We avoid talking about it at all costs. This allows the conversation to be dominated by white ethnic nationalists, and kooky news outlets on the far right. Which makes us even less likely to look at these issues honestly.

Getting into an argument on these topics with a Saudi is striking. A video I produced on the topic of Saudi ideology and Wahabi-ism yielded the same response from a couple of Saudi commenters. "Wahabi-ism doesn't exist!" was the gist of it. If pressed they would acknowledge the existence of Wahab, and the power that his approach has within Saudi Arabia. But there was no acknowledgement that this interpretation was anything other than the one true Islam. This demonstrates just how powerful oil money has made the Saudi interpretation. It's very possible for educated, well read, English speaking Wahabis to deny that any other alternative even exists.

It's time for that to change.

The Rest Of The Gulfies

Most Gulf countries exist due to forces similar to the ones that created Saudi Arabia. Western countries support backward Islamic

[74] https://cilisos.my/youd-never-guess-how-close-we-got-to-passing-hudud-in-malaysia-last-month/
[75] http://pointdebasculecanada.ca/saudi-religious-funding-fosters-terror-study-says/

fundamentalist sheiks precisely because of their weakness, not in spite of it. Countries like Qatar, the United Arab Emirates, Kuwait and Oman have all, to differing degrees, had a similar experience. The existence of most of these petty sheikdoms dates back to the British Empire, when their leaders got protection in return for providing welcoming ports for the British Navy. Petroleum wealth transformed their fortunes drastically. Where they once served as an imperialist bulwark against more powerful Islamic states like Ottoman Turkey and Persia, they now protected Western oil companies from the privations of Arab nationalists. They have also played a large part in the creation of international Jihadism, though it took the advent of the natural gas bonanza at the beginning of this century to turn most of them into real players.[76]

The recent impact of many of these countries, Qatar especially, has been disastrous. In some cases, Syria in particular, it's been even worse than that of the Saudis. But I'm generally leaving them out of this essay for four reasons. First, these places really are tiny, and their impact is likely to diminish in the new era of deflated petroleum prices. Second, there really are some positive things going on in most of them, enabled by their tiny populations. They have more space to evolve. Though radical Islam is a strong factor in most of their ideologies, they don't need it to control millions of people the way Saudi Arabia does. Third, because their power and influence is in many cases so recent it doesn't impact as much on the broader story of modern Islam I'm trying to convey here. And Fourth, I intend to write an essay here not a book, and I've got to limit the scope somewhere.

Conservative Islam Is Not Saudi Islam

Getting rid of Saudi funding won't solve the problem immediately. A lot of damage has been done. Due to Saudi educational systems, generations of children have now been brought up with some terrible ideas. Thankfully, this isn't as much of a problem as you'd think.

---

[76] Shadow Wars: The Secret Struggle for the Middle East by Christopher Davidson

There are signs of growing conservatism throughout the Islamic world. It can be easy to conflate this with radical terror, but that would be a mistake. There is an extremely low yield of terrorists for the hundreds of billions of dollars that the Saudis have put in to spreading their religion. It's a testament to the fundamental idiocy of their approach.

But the US Islamophobia industry reaches far beyond terrorism for its panicked propaganda. Everything from the adoption of Sharia law to the new prevalence of headscarves is seen as something to fight and freak out about. This broadening of the issue is unwise, and it also indicates a lack of awareness of a simple dynamic that is naturally making modern Islam more conservative.

The people of the Muslim world are getting richer, and, as we saw with Christianity in the 19th century, that includes a natural turn towards religion and conservatism. It does not create a natural turn towards wanting to kill people for your religion. Conservative Islam, like conservative Christianity, can be a nice complement to a bourgeoisie existence. If we look at what happened to Christianity in the 19th century, we can get a better sense of what's happening to Islam today.

Folks harbor a misconception about European and American history. During medieval times, we all huddled in our churches and did what the priests told us. Religious courts controlled much of daily life and family law. The conventional way of looking at what happened to this system is to just assume that the Reformation happened, then everybody got tolerant and enlightened and we moved towards today's cheerfully separated church and state in a very linear fashion. This couldn't be further from the truth. In fact, Christians spent most of the modern era getting more fervently religious. We've already discussed the fanaticism of the Reformation in the 16th and 17th centuries, but it didn't stop there.

Yes, the decades after the French Revolution at the dawn of the 1800s saw the end of "Christian Sharia" [77] across much of Europe, but that's not the whole story. Elite level changes in law and philosophy tend to make it into the history books, but that's not what was happening on the ground level at all.

To find out the truth, walk around a European or Northeast American city. If you look around a town in Europe, or the longer settled areas of the United States, you'll find that the majority of the churches were built in the 19th century. All the impressive central city cathedrals that you'd see on a city tour come from earlier periods, but all the outer district and suburban ones? They're pretty, but few of them are over 200 years old. A lot of medieval cathedrals were completely re-done in the 19th century too. The first thing any society does on its way to modernity is get religious.

Civilizations everywhere are built around religion. It's a crucial part of every phase of life in pre-modern cultures, and in many modern ones as well. Most Americans still get married in churches for example. Many Europeans do too, and I assure you most of those stained-glass windows don't date back to the 1400s. In both Islam and Christianity, one day of the week is dedicated to gathering in the communal house of faith and performing rituals. If you want to show your new wealth, you naturally do so by getting more serious about your traditional religion. Burgeoning mercantile wealth was the root of the Reformation zeal described above. Note that it was Northern Europe, which was getting rich off Atlantic and Asian trade that wanted to get more serious about religion, not Southern Europe, which was left with the decaying Mediterranean option.

The grandeur of a lot of these 19th century churches seems to conflict with the more humble aspirations of the 16th century founders of their sects. The Lutheran cathedral in Berlin ludicrously features gold statutes of Martin Luther, Philip Melancthon and the founding fathers of that

---

[77] Ecclesiastical courts are faaascinating, but beyond the scope of this essay. Basically, throughout European history the church had jurisdiction over a surprising amount of judicial matters. This didn't end until the 1700s and 1800s across most of Europe.

particular Protestant strain. If those 16th century guys had any consistency at all they'd be appalled. Theology rarely gets in the way of display. This too highlights an interesting development. Religious fanaticism tends to moderate itself over time, if left to develop on its own. We can see this happening in Iran today. This dynamic is the reason I'm less worried about Sharia in Aceh, Indonesia than most.

This process of wealth leading to more religion rather than less is very well illustrated by Saudi Arabia. Most readers of this essay will be familiar with the grim picture of life in "modern" Saudi Arabia. Almost all forms of entertainment are banned. Social life across genders outside of the family is banned. Women are subjected to an extreme form of repression, unable to drive, and unable to appear in public without a related male escort. Many women spend the majority of their lives within their family compounds, under what strikes the western reader as a form of house arrest.[78] Fanatical religious police patrol the streets, ready to pounce on the slightest variation from these requirements. The justification for all this is that they are trying to live life as Muhammad did. You'd think that this style of life dated back centuries…

Not so much.

In fact, it was impossible to support this lifestyle before oil revenues began in the 1930s, and even before they really heated up in the 1970s. Taking half of your population out of public and economic life is expensive. Just a few decades back, life in Saudi Arabia was very different. As Karen Elliot House says…

> … Saudi was much freer in the late 1970s for both Saudi and Western women. In those days, most Western women, including me, rarely wore an abaya [the full head to toe black covering], and I was often invited to mixed gender dinners in the homes of Saudi officials. Now an abaya is essential to avoid unwanted attention, and

[78] House's <u>On Saudi Arabia</u> provides chilling documentation of all of this.

> Saudi women are much rarer than alcohol at dinner, even in the homes of elite businessmen and government officials. [79]

Saudi is an extreme case of course. Its limitless revenues and malignant ideology make it different. But this example highlights a broader trend. As literacy, education, and the ability to make choices beyond subsistence has spread in the Islamic world, so has religious conservatism. This is natural, not something to be feared. It wouldn't surprise me if broader Islamic culture swung back in the coming decades. The turn to religion is part of the status and virtue signaling that we all spend a lot of our lives performing. It's fashion really.

Some people of course choose to react to all this ostentation by attempting to get back to the roots of the religion. This could be seen in the renewal of 19th century Christian monasticism, and it can be seen in the rise of Salafism in the Islamic world today. Salafists want to live in the time of the prophet. But this ideology is not necessarily violent. It can include the same largely pacifist turning toward god that Christian monasticism does. Yes, there is support for jihadi Salafism in the Koran, but the very temporal aims of the Saudi and US government in Afghanistan, Syria and throughout the Muslim world were what pushed people towards killing. The current strain of murderous Jihadism is a product of Saudi-American cooperation against the Soviet Union and Bashar Assad.

And yes, success in modernization can drive some marginal people towards more extreme ideologies. Tunisia is both the only Arab country to emerge from the Arab Spring with a (so-far) successful modern democracy, and it is also the largest exporter of ISIS fighters by a large margin.

But on balance, it's worth saying again, new money makes people want to consume religious goods and do so more ostentatiously, not blow themselves up. It is the widening of Islamic prosperity that has made

[79] House Loc.1300

religious law, a more restrictive view of female life, and scriptural literalism and proselytization popular. 19th century European and American prosperity did the exact same thing to Christianity.

In the Victorian era, economic development provided new opportunities for women, but it also provided new opportunities for repression. The "Cult of Domesticity" argued that a woman's place was in the home. New wealth gave husbands and fathers the ability to enforce this notion, as well as the ability to more fiercely enforce older notions of chastity and "honor". The same tension can be seen across the Islamic world today, where women have new opportunities, and a newly well-funded patriarchal religion to deal with. Muslim women like Tansu Çiller and Benazir Bhutto become prime ministers, while in Saudi Arabia women can no longer eat dinner with their husband's guests. The playing out of these forces shaped 20th century America, and continue to do so today. In 1920, the same year that women got the vote, the United States embarked on a religiously inspired 13-year experiment with alcohol prohibition. That experiment failed disastrously. Women and tolerance won out in the West, and I am confident that they will do so in the Islamic world as well.

If you look at this history, the majority of Islamophobic discourse, from Bill Maher to Breitbart and Michael Flynn, looks deeply silly. In their minds, something about Islam or the Koran is fundamentally broken, and a clash of civilizations is inevitable. It's been going on for over a thousand years after all! But what we're dealing with now hasn't been with us for millennia. It's barely been here for decades.

The practice of Islam is a tremendously complex phenomenon, playing out across dozens of countries and within 1.6 billion minds. Any narrative we construct around it, including this one, is going to be limited in its explanatory power. The practice of Islam is moving in different directions as we speak. Here's an example…

Are you familiar with Tinder? It's among the lower lows in mating technology we've concocted on our slouch to Gomorrah. It does away with the pretense that you have any interest in what a person has to say for him or herself and simply presents a picture. If the aesthetics are enticing you swipe right, if not left. As loathsome as all this is, I am a single man, and I participate. In Turkey, where I lived for five years, I would often come across women wearing hijabs.

One picture in particular struck me. She looked off into the distance, as if contemplating the wall to my right, as she cradled her head with a hand holding a lit cigarette, careful not to brush it against her headscarf. Here you have the two elements that get the lion's share of attention in current analysis of Turkey and its place in the world. The urge to return to traditional Islamic piety represented by the headscarf. The difficulty of doing so represented by this ostensibly conservative woman's presence on a dating website, and what strikes me as a provocative choice to pose with a cigarette in an elegant subversion of some views of Islamic femininity (She swiped left…).

Islam's turn towards conservatism is happening in the context of societies that are getting much richer, and people are trying to figure out what it means to be both Muslim and modern. My time in Turkey convinced me that no matter how malign certain political elements are, Muslim individuals are going to make their own choices about what Islam means. It is not a process to be feared.

But that process will take longer if we continue to turn a blind eye to Saudi efforts. The tremendous economic imbalance between the Gulf States and the rest of the Islamic world has allowed an angry intolerant Islam to become the "official" world form. Saudi Arabia has invested tens of billions of dollars in pushing the ideological balance of Islam to the precipice of radicalism. It has been able to do this because of its status as a US protectorate. But the ideology alone wasn't enough. To push handfuls of young Muslims over that precipice of radicalism into jihadi terrorism you need politics.

POLITICS

It is the unnatural bargain between Saudi Arabia and the United States that has provided the political justification for Islamic terrorism. Saudi Arabia's eagerness to serve US interests has led to both stages of the metastasis of Jihadi ideology. This is the root of "what's going on" with Islam. Pretending to talk about terrorism without reckoning with US and Saudi policy is indefensible. Islam is not the problem. The problem is what Saudi and US policies have done to Islam. But we just don't talk about Saudi Arabia in the United States.

1910s-1960s

As I've mentioned above, Saudi Arabia's main virtue from the British and American perspective is its weakness. Prior to the oil billions the Saudi royal family held no real attraction for the broader Arab world. Countries based in urban centers like Cairo and Damascus saw the development of Arab nationalism in the late 19th and early 20th centuries. These countries, and especially the ideology of Pan-Arabism, presented a prickly problem for the Western powers. It led to attempts to unify all Arab countries, with Egypt and Syria briefly creating a United Arab Republic under Nasser between 1958 and 1961. North Africa has seen a variety of less serious attempts. The United States felt threatened by these moves. Arab nationalists were impertinent enough to think that their oil resources belonged to the Arab peoples rather than foreign oil companies. The solution here was to support more traditional monarchies in oil exporting areas, like the Sauds and those running other Gulf countries like Kuwait and the UAE.

The Saudi balancing act made that regime particularly attractive. Their medieval set up and religious fundamentalism was occasionally embarrassing, but it made it likely that they'd never present a real threat to the orderly transfer of oil resources to the west. It's a lot easier to keep a royal court happy than it is to keep an entire people happy, whether those people are organized as a democracy or as a nationalist dictatorship. The

Saudis' dismal military performance has proven the wisdom of this choice in one sense. Saudi Arabia's massive military procurement has left it with one of the most well equipped militaries in the world. On paper. Their inability to actually use those resources has been proven again and again, from their desperation in the face of the Iraqi threat in the 1990s to their brutal and failing war in Yemen today. Through idle flattery and gifts, exemplified by FDR's meeting with Ibn Saud on Bitter Lake in 1945, this dependence was masked as an "Alliance". But dependence is what it has always been, by design.

Saudi Arabia would not have been founded without British support. Without US support it would not have lasted as long as it has. In different periods, Western support shielded the country from very real threats from Jordanian Hashemites, Egyptian nationalists, Iraqi Baathists, and Iranian Shia. It may not look like it, but if you read the country's history it's hard to avoid the suspicion that Saudi Arabia is an American protectorate, or even a colony.

1970-1980s

In the late 1970s a number of factors led to the implementation of an idea that had been floating around the US military industrial complex for decades.[80] A little appreciated fact of modern Russia is that it holds the largest Islamic population of any European country. The figures are disputed but Russia's Muslim population currently stands at somewhere between 14 to 20% of the whole.[81] The Soviet Union, which incorporated the Muslim states of Azerbaijan, Kazakhstan, Kyrgyzstan, Uzbekistan, and Tajikistan was more heavily Islamic.

Earlier in the cold war, elements of the CIA and a Russian émigré promoted the idea that the USSR's Muslim population could be used

---

[80] Davidson pps. 101-105

[81] Different sources quote different numbers. An exact read is difficult because of standard Russian obfuscation, and the large migrant population from the 'stans that gravitates to Moscow and other Russian cities for economic opportunity

against the Soviet state.[82] This strategy was seen as a way to both guard the Middle East against Communism, and undermine the Soviet Union on its home turf. Of course, to do this, the Muslim population had to get a lot more fervent about religion. Saudi Arabia was the obvious partner to help bring this about. The Saudi Regime's need to promote Wahabism abroad to placate the Ulema dovetailed nicely with US interests.

Interestingly, the 1970s saw Saudi Arabia's first serious actions against US interests. Saudi Arabia's creation of the first oil shock in 1973 contributed to the derailing of the US economy for much of the decade. This should have prompted a re-thinking of the US-Saudi relationship, but Cold War realities made that impossible.

The Soviet occupation of Afghanistan in 1979 opened a malign, if useful, new dimension in US-Saudi cooperation. To fight that war the CIA, in partnership with the Pakistani and Saudi intelligence services, built a world-wide Jihadi network. This is what became Al Queda, and what eventually led to the fall of the Twin Towers on September 11th 2001. The creation of this trans-national Jihadi network would not have been as successful without the world-wide US policy of encouraging fundamentalist Islam. We knew exactly what we were doing. Figures such as Jimmy Carter's National Security Advisor Zbigniew Brzezinski[83] and Reagan's Secretary of Defense Caspar Weinberger[84] are on record as acknowledging the pursuit of this policy in Afghanistan. Additionally, there is evidence that we consciously supported the most viciously fundamentalist aspects of the Afghan insurgency.[85]

The machine that the US and Saudi Arabia built up to fight the war in Afghanistan was impossible to limit to one country's battlefield. Individuals from throughout the Muslim world were recruited and radicalized for the purpose. Those that survived were always going to go

[82] Davidson p. 103
[83] Davidson p. 102
[84] Davidson p. 104
[85] Davidson p. 104

home with a set of fundamentalist and Jihadi ideas and goals. I suspect that the United States had no interest in limiting these effects, though proof of this is understandably hard to find. The interests of our partners however are not in dispute. They wanted this virus to spread.

From the start Pakistan's Inter-Service Intelligence (ISI) wanted to use fundamentalists from the Afghan war in its decades old battle with India over Kashmir. The Pakistani leaders of the 1980s probably did not anticipate how much damage this policy would do to their own country, but it's not clear they've fully reversed course even today. Saudi Arabia treated the Afghan war as an expansion of its policy of world-wide Wahabization. The Afghani and Wahabi missions were supported by the same "charitable" institutions, like the Muslim World League and the International Islamic Relief Organization. In fact, they were the same mission. In country after country the same offices were used to change Islam locally and recruit soldiers for the Afghan war.

You'd think that the spread of hyper-conservative Islamic radicals and thought would be something that a secular republic like the United States would question, or even try to discourage. Because of the Cold War however, the spread of Wahabism was something that the United States actively promoted and facilitated. This is true whether it was conscious or not. I'm fairly confident that it was conscious.

This policy was more successful than most realize. Everybody knows that our Jihadists kicked the USSR out of Afghanistan in 1989. But how many people are aware of this policy's other "successes"? From 1992 to 1997, Tajikstan, a former Soviet Republic, experienced a bloody civil war, largely driven by Wahabi Islam, that killed up to 100,000 people (1-1.5% of the population). Militants returning from Afghanistan also destabilized another formerly Soviet aligned country in the 1990s. The Algerian civil war killed as many as 150,000 people between 1991 and 2001. It's unlikely that many tears were shed at the CIA for Algeria's formally socialist government. The current plight of Chechnya, a formerly breakaway province of Russia, also owes a lot to US-Saudi cooperation on Jihadism. Though the initial supporters of independence in the 1990s may have been more secular, Wahabism's influence over the separatists grew steadily.

Formerly Soviet Jihadists remain some of the most fearsome soldiers of ISIS on Mesopotamia's battlegrounds to this day. 2017 opened with a horrific attack on a nightclub in Istanbul, Turkey, a city I called home for five years. The perpetrator was from Uzbekistan.[86] This too can be seen as a result of the US-Saudi link. When Vladimir Putin accuses the United States of cooperating with Jihadists, this is not just propaganda. It is the fruit of decades of experience.

1990s-September 11th 2001

Throughout the 1990s, handfuls of people in the US government realized that they had created a monster, and took steps to try to stop it. At every stage these steps were stymied by the centrality of the US-Saudi relationship. CIA teams were looking into ways to kill or capture Osama Bin Laden, but they wanted to do it without offending his allies in the Taliban. The Taliban were strongly supported by our "allies" the Saudis.[87]

After the cold war and the fall of the Soviet Union, real common ground between Saudi Arabia and the United States was hard to find. Both countries still had a grudge against Iran. Saudi Arabia was, and is terrified by the prospect of an American change in attitude towards their much more sophisticated and historically powerful rival. Iran's more honest stabs at democratization, and highly developed civil society make it a more natural ally of the United States, but the Saudi connection now has decades of history behind it.

Much has been made of the relationships between the Bush family and the Saudi royal family. That mutually enriching relationship does exist, as it does with the Clintons and the Trumps, but no matter what people say, the

---

[86] https://en.wikipedia.org/wiki/2017_Istanbul_nightclub_shooting
[87] Ghost Wars Steve Coll

United States is not yet a dynastic monarchy. The power of the Bush family alone is not enough to keep the Saudi connection going. The relationship with the Saudis extends across party lines, and deep into the machinery of the US government. Generations of professionals in the intelligence community have worked closely with their Saudi counterparts. Many of those Saudi counterparts, and the princes above them, have been educated in US universities, and are experts in acting differently in different contexts. Georgetown educated Prince Turki al Faisal, who ran the Saudi intelligence service for decades, was known to have a drink or two with his American allies if the context was right.[88] Prince Bandar Bin Sultan, the long-time US ambassador was also an expert at showing a modern face while acting on behalf of a distinctly medieval state. The real bonds of affection between these men and the men and women of the US government have helped keep the relationship going long after any outside observer could see that the effects were horrible.

What About the Petrodollar!?!?

Many point to the "Petrodollar" thesis to explain the continued US relationship with the Saudis. The theory maintains that Saudi Arabia holds incredible power over the US because it chooses to sell its oil in dollars. This supposedly explains all manner of US mistakes. On the wilder fringes of the internet, you can find people claiming that the fall of Iraq's Saddam Hussein, and The Shah of Iran can be traced to their threats to stop trading oil in dollars.

I don't buy this strong version of the Petrodollar thesis. Generally, if I most often see a theory expressed in angry, all-caps YouTube comments, I feel safe ignoring that theory. But it's worth looking at the claim in detail, as laid down by one of its more literate supporters. According to Jerry Robinson of the website Follow the Money…

---

[88] Ghost Wars Steve Coll

> …thanks to the petrodollar system, growing global demand for oil leads to an increase in U.S. dollar demand. This artificial demand for U.S. dollars has provided remarkable benefits for the U.S. economy… The problem with this situation is that the only way that it can be sustained is if the demand for the dollar and for U.S. debt securities remains consistently strong.[89]

That's not crazy. The US dollar is certainly effected by its status as the world's reserve currency, and Gulf investments play a significant role in shoring that up. But that does not mean that the loss of Saudi dollar transactions would be catastrophic for the US dollar and US power in the current environment. The standard argument against this scenario is that it could never happen.

Saudi Arabia and the United States are too intertwined for the action to be plausible. A change in the arrangement would supposedly be mutually assured destruction. The Saudi royal family is not viable without US support, and its members have been investing their winnings in the US market for decades. The Saudi Regime's investments in the US are their insurance policy. Pulling their support from the US economy would most likely leave them without a country to profit from, and with a pile of depreciating Euros and Renminbi to invest in a disintegrating world economy.

This standard argument dictates that the US needs to continue its policy of covering for Saudi Arabia. Heck, if the relationship survived 9/11 it should be able to survive anything, right?

Wrong.

The relationship is not sustainable, because the current regime in Saudi Arabia is not sustainable. Sooner or later the current regime is going to disintegrate, and no matter what the nature of the new regime is, it's not

[89] https://en.wikipedia.org/wiki/List_of_countries_by_oil_production

going to be friendly to the United States. I would argue that this is in fact the best possible moment to unwind the Saudi petrodollar issue.

As of Spring 2017, Saudi Arabia is in an unprecedentedly weak position, and there is no real alternative to the dollar as reserve currency.

With the fall in the price of oil, and the explosion in diversity of petroleum sources over the past few decades, Saudi Arabia now accounts for a smaller share of dollar transactions than it ever has. I believe this trend will continue. But even if it doesn't, now is a good time to jump off the Saudi train. If the royal family is about to fall, we get to leave on our own terms. If the Saudi royal family lasts, we may not be as free to act in a few years or decades.

For the dollar to lose its reserve currency status there needs to be an alternative. At this point, though, there isn't one. The Euro and the Chinese Renminbi are the most plausible alternatives. But the prospects of both currencies are even less stable than the dollar in the current environment. China's growth engine is faltering, and the European Union is a mess. More traditional alternatives, like the British Pound, and the Swiss Franc, are also rooted in a deeply uncertain Europe.[90] The fundamentals of the Yen and the Japanese economy are also completely up in the air. It is possible that one of these currencies will emerge as a plausible alternative in the coming decade. So it may be a good idea to act now.

At this point, a Saudi Arabia sized loss in dollar transactions would not destroy the value of the US dollar. There is no hidden logic to continued US support for Saudi Arabia. Since the 1990s we've gotten little in return other than tragedy.

---

[90] The Swiss Franc is the most plausible alternative reserve currency. But the Swiss have no interest in that status, and are working hard against it. They have maintained a negative interest rate for over a year now, and will likely continue to do so for the foreseeable future. https://www.ft.com/content/bcc092fc-7743-11e6-a0c6-39e2633162d5

9/11

So did the Saudis do 9/11?

It's quite a question. And after 9/11 the US government's main priority was to avoid answering it.[91] Washington, DC's goal has been misdirection, and the preservation of our Saudi protectorate. This was the main goal of the "Islam is a Religion of Peace" mantra that George W. Bush launched in the days following the attack.

For 14 years, the US government refused to release the 28 pages of the joint congressional inquiry into the 9/11 attacks that discussed the support that the hijackers received from Saudi government officials and members of the Saudi Royal family.[92] When the still redacted pages were finally released in July of 2016, interest levels were low. They illustrate many connections, though they do so in vague and carefully guarded terms. The report documents numerous meetings, and extensive support for the hijackers from Saudi government officials and intelligence officers.[93] The pages make for shocking reading even today. Had they been released in 2002, there might have been serious repercussions. But we've moved on.

It's worth mentioning that had Iran been proved to have a small fraction of these connections to the 9/11 hijackers, Tehran would have been a smoking crater by mid-2002.

British academic Christopher Davidson has highlighted that the 28 pages don't represent the full base of knowledge about these connections. More information has since come to light. Freedom of Information Act requests have revealed FBI information that never made it to Congressional investigators. An adviser to a nephew of the Saudi king owned a house in Sarasota Florida. The family living there had numerous contacts with the hijackers who were training nearby. The house was completely

---

[91] Davidson pps. 153-156
[92] http://www.newyorker.com/news/daily-comment/twenty-eight-pages
[93] https://28pages.org/the-declassified-28-pages/

abandoned two weeks prior to 9/11.[94] The Prince in question was one of a number of Saudis that the Bush administration flew out of the country on September 13th, when most other travel was still shut down.[95] These figures were shielded from any further investigation. Many of them conveniently died, or were reported to have died, once they returned to Saudi Arabia.[96]

With this flight, and other acts and omissions we'll never hear about, the US government guaranteed that we'll never know the full truth. It's left to obscure academics and lawyers to try to piece together the facts. We'll never know.

Did Crown Prince Abdullah[97] decree that 9/11 should happen? Almost certainly not. But we can still say with confidence that Saudi Arabia was responsible for 9/11.

15 of the 19 hijackers were from Saudi Arabia, and were products of that country's depraved educational system. Al Queda, the organization responsible for the attack, was led by a Saudi Arabian, and grew out of the US-Saudi war in Afghanistan. Al Queda was founded by a diverse group of radicals, but they were all raised on a stew of ideas and were educated in institutions with funding that came straight from Saudi Arabia. Beyond the top-level decision makers, it's clear that there was a good deal of support for Al Queda within Saudi Arabia. Reports from after the attacks indicate that as much as 80% of the security services[98], and 95% of young Saudi men sympathized with the group.[99] As documented above, Saudi charities were deeply intertwined with violent radicals in Al Queda and beyond. Elements of the Saudi Government supported the

---

94 Davidson pps. 158-159

95 http://investigations.nbcnews.com/_news/2012/03/14/10672374-new-questions-about-fbi-probe-of-saudis-post-911-exodus

96 Davidson p. 159

97 Abdullah became Saudi Arabia's King in 2005 on the death of his half-brother King Fahd (r.1982-2005). Fahd was debilitated by a stroke in 1995. As Crown Prince and Regent from 1995 to 2005 Abdullah ruled the country in fact if not in name.

98 Davidson p. 153

99 Gold p. 207

hijackers once they arrived in the United States. Incredibly, elements of the Saudi religious hierarchy openly celebrated the attacks in the fall of 2001.[100] These voices were soon silenced, but the fact that they existed at all is telling.

Without Saudi Arabia there would not have been a 9/11. Period.

When you consider that we know as much as we do, in spite of US government obstruction, it seems very likely that more serious elements of the Saudi government than we are aware of directly supported 9/11.[101]

The Saudi Blind Spot

Reading about these 15-year old connections and actions is tremendously frustrating. It's clear to me that had any of these leads been investigated properly, we'd have a much clearer idea of who truly bears the responsibility for 9/11. The problem was that they weren't investigated. Whenever Saudi Arabians were involved the gears of justice ground to a halt. The FBI and other agencies became less interested in investigating things fully.[102] Saudi government explanations are quickly accepted, with no further evidence required. This doesn't just apply to government, it applies to US journalism as well.[103] It's as if there's a "Saudi Blind Spot", in which any crimes attributable to that country simply disappear. It's deeply frustrating that this attitude persists in the wake of 9/11.

This "Blind Spot" operates in the aggregate, and it also applies to individual incidents. Researching this essay has been maddening. Through a combination of the urge not to seem politically incorrect, and I suspect a lot of direct and indirect Saudi pressure, Saudi Arabia's impact on Islam is little discussed. All the think tanks that one would hope would look into these issues are mute. This may have something to do with the

[100] Gold. Pps 186-190
[101] Davidson pps. 156-159
[102] http://investigations.nbcnews.com/_news/2012/03/14/10672374-new-questions-about-fbi-probe-of-saudis-post-911-exodus
[103] https://www.youtube.com/watch?v=F3muUDK7kel

fact that these organizations are largely "pay to play" outfits,[104] and Gulf countries are large consumers that it does not pay to offend. Academia and respectable journalism also avoids this topic like the plague. Annoyingly, the majority of the coverage comes from unsavory outlets like Breitbart and other right wing or Christian fundamentalist news sources. These outlets are easy to ignore. On most issues, many of them should be ignored. It's tragic that this all-important topic has been relegated to the fever swamps.

The incident that comes most clearly to mind is the San Bernardino attacks at the end of 2015.
On December 2nd, 2015, a mentally disturbed couple killed 14 people in the name of Islam. I am not a fan of conspiracy theories, but it's very difficult to describe the coverage of Saudi Arabia's relationship to this event as anything other than a cover-up.

Most accounts mentioned Saudi Arabia, but they only did it once, usually towards the bottom of the article. This is an odd choice. The female shooter was raised in Saudi Arabia. She did go to university in Pakistan, but afterwards she moved back. In Pakistani news sources she was described as a "Saudi Girl".[105] She met her husband, the other San Bernardino shooter, in Saudi Arabia, and that is almost certainly where they were both radicalized. A Wahabi mosque in Pakistan was also important in the female shooter's journey to lunacy. She may have spent a few years of her life outside of Saudi Arabia, but Saudi religion was always with her. The stories all mentioned Saudi Arabia briefly, but then try to switch the focus to visa procedures, or Syrian refugees or gun control or anything else at all really.[106] They want us to look at anything other than the elephant in the room.

---

104 https://www.nytimes.com/2014/09/07/us/politics/foreign-powers-buy-influence-at-think-tanks.html

105 http://tribune.com.pk/story/1005544/tashfeen-malik-was-a-saudi-girl-who-stood-out-at-a-pakistani-university/

106 A particularly egregious example of this coverage can be found in this Washington Post Article from December 7th, 2015. https://www.washingtonpost.com/news/post-nation/wp/2015/12/07/san-bernardino-officials-say-they-are-trying-to-resume-normal-business-after-shooting/?utm_term=.a49961e01d40 I somewhat intemperately covered this issue in a video entitled "Trump, the San Bernardino Cover Up, and Saudi Arabia" https://www.youtube.com/watch?v=F3muUDK7keI

This is nothing new. Every significant terror attack this century has had large Saudi involvement. The Paris attacks in November 2015 were planned in Saudi-funded mosques in Belgium. 15 of the 19 9/11 hijackers were Saudis. The June 2016 attack in Orlando, Florida was carried out by an Afghani-American who spent his entire religious life swimming in a sea of Wahabi nonsense. As this essay was being finalized, a British citizen attacked the UK Parliament, killing five people. He lived and worked in Saudi Arabia from 2005-2009.[107] Allow me to say that again. *Every significant terror attack this century has had large Saudi involvement*. This is ignored, over and over again.

Rather than blame the country and the ideology that is actually responsible for these attacks, everybody from Fox News to Barack Obama pretends that Saudi Arabia has nothing to do with it. This is a terrible mistake.

In 2016 the State Department issued a report labeling Iran as the world's largest supporter of Terror. In the same report they also pointed out that ISIS was the largest threat.[108] This is bonkers. Iran does a lot more to fight ISIS than the United States does. Iran is portrayed as the largest supporter of Terrorism because of its support for Iraqi militias and Hezbollah, two organizations who have spent the majority of their time over the past couple years combating Wahabi influenced radicals. To be sure, Hezbollah fires rockets into Israel, which is terrible. But the majority of the fighting and dying that Hezbollah does today takes place on the fields of Syria and Iraq. It is working to defend the governments of Syria and Iraq. Defining this work as "Terrorism" is absurd.

One of the most insidious things about the "Saudi Blind Spot" is the way that it turns Islamophobes into eager propagandists for Saudi Arabia. Saudi Arabia desperately wants to convince the world that their version of Islam is the one true Islam. So do Western Islamophobes. This is true across the spectrum, including both the openly bigoted people on the

[107] http://www.telegraph.co.uk/news/2017/03/24/khalid-masood-everything-know-london-attacker/
[108] http://www.cnn.com/2016/06/02/politics/state-department-report-terrorism/

streets and on Twitter, and supposedly more "liberal" and "rational" folks like Sam Harris and Bill Maher. The inability of these people to talk seriously about Saudi Arabia is extraordinarily frustrating. In a conversation in early 2017 Harris and Maher sat down to discuss Trump's first executive order on Muslim immigration.[109] They mentioned Boko Haram, Al Queda, and ISIS, and discussed the "War of Ideas" in Islam. Saudi Arabia came up once, but the conversation was quickly diverted to a rant on Burqas and "centuries of brainwashing".

It hasn't been centuries of brainwashing. As I've documented above, it has been decades of brainwashing. By refusing to talk about Wahabism, and by talking about all Islam as if it is the same thing as Saudi Wahabism, Harris and Maher are enthusiastic participants in that brainwashing. This is great for Saudi Arabia. When the question becomes the West vs. Islam, rather than the West vs. Saudi Arabia, Saudi Arabia gets about 1.5 billion allies they don't deserve. Islamophobes themselves are eager participants in this cover up of the true problem with modern Islam.

This cover up has real costs. Despite respectable media's foolish choice not to engage seriously with any of these issues, the average citizen in the West can plainly see the contradictions. "How is it that we've made no progress against Radical Islam in 15 years?" "How can this be a religion of peace?" By protecting Saudi Arabia, our leaders deflect the anger and frustration of John Q. Public onto the entire religion. This emphasis had pernicious effects long before the Trump Administration.

In the aftermath of the San Bernardino attacks Congress enacted, and Obama signed into law the *Visa Waiver Program Improvement and Terrorist Travel Prevention Act of 2015*[110]. This law makes it more difficult for people to travel into the United States without visas if they have visited Iraq, Syria, or "any other country or area of concern"[111]. Iran, Libya, Somalia, Yemen, and Sudan were quickly added to the list of no-

[109] https://www.youtube.com/watch?v=LV7eVvph69Y
[110] https://homeland.house.gov/wp-content/uploads/2015/12/HR158_Miller.pdf
[111] https://homeland.house.gov/wp-content/uploads/2015/12/HR158_Miller.pdf

go countries.[112] Notice anything about that list? There's no mention of Saudi Arabia, Afghanistan or Pakistan, the sources and preferred travel destinations of the vast majority of actual terrorists who have carried out actions in the United States. I don't support this measure in any case, but the fact that the legislation intended to "stop another San Bernardino" doesn't touch the countries that radicalized the San Bernardino attackers would be hilarious if it wasn't so tragic.

If this list looks familiar, it's because it's the same list Trump used in his abortive "Refugee Ban" in early 2017. Trump's action was far more sweeping. The Obama restriction simply required visas for those who had traveled to those countries, regardless of their nationality. A British friend of mine, who had traveled to Iraq for diplomatic purposes, was blocked from visiting the United States, for example, because she wasn't aware of the new requirements. I found Obama's action to be wrong, and deeply silly, but Trump's approach is on another level entirely.

Trump's action specifically targets all nationals from these countries, blocking their access to the United States, no matter what visas or vetting they had received. Ludicrously, the action initially targeted legal permanent residents of the United States as well. By using the same silly list Obama used for his earlier action, Trump was serving the Saudi idea that Islam and Christianity are locked in some sort of "Clash of Civilizations". While also leaving Saudi nationals out of the order.

The "Saudi Blind Spot" is real, and it is making us less safe.

2001-2011
The "War On Terror"

[112] https://homeland.house.gov/press/mccaul-miller-on-further-travel-restrictions-for-visa-waiver-program/

The War On Terror is a joke. On 9/11 we were attacked by Saudis, working for an organization run by a Saudi, funded by Saudis, and in service to Saudi Islam.

In his State of the Union address in January 2002, George W. Bush announced our plans for the
"War on Terror". Saudi Arabia was not mentioned once in this "Axis of Evil" Speech. You know who did get a mention though? Saudi Arabia's two greatest enemies, Iraq and Iran. We essentially declared war on both countries.

The horrific farce that is the US invasion of Iraq quickly drove the US closer to the Saudis. There was very limited thinking about what would come next. Iraq is majority Shia, which meant that despite declaring war on Iran with the "Axis of Evil" speech, we gave them an incredible gift by toppling Saddam. The insurgency that grew up had both Sunni and Shia elements. Both elements had a murderous effect on US soldiers. As is often emphasized the Shia insurgency had the direct support of Iran. What is less emphasized is the fact that the Sunni insurgency had significant support from Saudi Arabia and the other Gulf countries. And the US helped.

When the US woke up to the fact that they had created a satellite state for Iran, they became a lot more interested in helping fund the Sunni elements that were left in the country. Washington, DC knew that Saudi money was killing US soldiers, but they didn't know which Saudi money was doing it. And if we had acted to shut the whole stream of funding down, as we should have after 9/11, we would have given more power to Iran and the Shia Iraqis.

This was the start of the ridiculous game we continue to play in Syria, Iraq and Yemen today. In the effort to counter Iran, we facilitate Gulf funding of radical elements in all three countries. We attempt to pick the "good guys" even though the funding going to all elements comes packaged with Wahabi fundamentalism. Sometimes it works out OK, but it usually doesn't. The temporary success of the "Iraqi surge" in 2008 and 2009 is a good example. Much was made of the "Sunni Awakening" that saw the temporary end of the Sunni insurgency in Iraq.

We now know that it didn't end, it just went underground. Its quick recovery happened long before the fall of Mosul to ISIS in 2014. The Iraqi territories "pacified" by the Sunni Awakening, have all had to be retaken over the past few years, at a great cost in lives and treasure. The toxic soup of Wahabi thought and arms also contributed to the growth of ISIS, with horrible consequences we are all very familiar with.

Yet Rudy Giuliani and the US government continue to insist that Saudi Arabia is a worthwhile partner in the War on Terror. This assertion comes from the close anti-Iran partnership between the two countries, but it also draws support from one historical event. Between 2004 and 2005 Al Queda took its war to Saudi Arabia. A series of large scale terrorist attacks wracked the kingdom. This did prompt a serious reevaluation from the Saudi government. Mass arrests of Al Queda operatives and sympathizers took place for the first time. Some thought was given towards cutting out the "Go out and Kill People" elements of religious instruction in Saudi Arabia and abroad.

This episode is often mentioned as the point at which Saudi Arabia changed for the better. But the vast majority of the country's ideology and international outreach remains unchanged. Sure there's less outright support for violent Jihad. But all the other steps of the Wahabi radicalization process still receive enthusiastic and growing Saudi support. Radical Islamic groups that don't advocate actions against the West and Saudi Arabia still receive state support. The US media has put a great deal of effort into portraying these elements in Syria as "moderates" and "good guys". The individuals in these groups, in Syria and Iraq in particular, easily move between "Good Guy" groups like the Free Syrian Army, and "Bad Guy" groups like ISIS or the Jihadists formerly known as Al Nusra. It's an easy switch to make, because the underlying ideologies are very, very similar. Saudi Arabia is not a worthwhile partner. For anything really.

2011-2017
The Arab Spring, Syria and ISIS

The Arab Spring's very predictable fall into a Jihadi mess in multiple countries is also a product of Saudi and other Gulf influence. I still believe that the Arab Spring was a positive development. A couple decades from now it should be remembered as a massive step forward. Unfortunately, as many revolutions do, it first functioned to create a vacuum. The most motivated and organized groups were the ones that profited. From the 1920s through 1989, these groups were usually Communist thanks to Soviet funding and propaganda. In the Islamic world today, thanks to Gulf funding, these groups are now Islamist. There is a wide spectrum of Islamist thought, and as mentioned above, some of the swing towards conservatism is quite legitimate and natural. The failure of Mohammed Morsi's completely unready for prime time Muslim Brotherhood government in Egypt is probably something to be lamented. The true horror of Saudi, and other Gulf influence is revealed in Syria.

In 2011, assorted groups, some liberal, some Islamist, and all justified, rose up against Bashar Assad, the Syrian dictator. The US government has a long memory. In many ways it is still motivated by cold war priorities, simply because nobody has taken the time to develop new ones.[113] Witness the quarter century of pointless moves against Russia that finally bore fruit in the Ukraine crisis of 2014 and a renewed mini Cold War. Syria is another example. The Assad family's decades old alignment with the Soviet Union is still the most important thing about that regime in US government eyes. Never mind the fact that the Soviet Union is decades dead, and that Russia's sole overseas base, located in Syria, has little strategic value. An opportunity to take down Assad was not to be missed! Unlike the revolutions against Egypt's Mubarak and the Tunisian and

[113] I'm working on it.

Bahraini rulers, the US government was quick to offer full-throated support.

As 2011 wore on, and Assad continued to fail to fall as easily as predicted, the United States decided to go back to the same plan it had used in Afghanistan in the 1980s. Turkey maps pretty clearly to Pakistan in this example, though Turkey has managed to preserve a greater degree of stability thus far.[114] Saudi Arabia, now joined to a much larger extent by the other Gulf monarchies, would provide the same massive funding and support to the revolutionaries. Just as it did in the 1980s, this support would come with strings attached. The multifarious groups fighting against the Assad regime knew that they could receive greater funding the more closely they adhered to a strictly Jihadi line. This gibed well with an already extant move towards Islamic conservatism among the Sunni Syrian people. As noted above, people who are getting richer want to be more religious, but it takes politics to make them kill. Assad provided the reason for and the Gulf states provided the money for radicalization.

Most US talking heads seem to be in agreement that Obama "didn't do enough" in Syria. This is just plain wrong. He did too much. The jihadization of the Syrian revolution would not have been possible without US support. Turkey would not have facilitated the travel of foreign fighters, and Saudi Arabia and the Gulf states would not have poured in their billions without some degree of approval from the United States. Our government was very publicly committed to Assad's fall, and equally committed to not using US military assets to bring it about. From 2011-on, acknowledged or not, re-running the 1980s battle for Afghanistan in contemporary Syria has been US policy.

Despite its horrific consequences I think it's still possible to take an ambivalent view of the CIA sponsored birth of international Jihadism in 1980s Afghanistan. The Soviet Union, even in the 1980s, was an existential threat to the United States. The 1980s were a much more

[114] The growing civil war in Turkey's southeast prompts the question of how long this can last.

dangerous time, and every tool was necessary to fight a truly international war. US and Soviet proxies were fighting very hot wars on multiple continents and in at least nine countries.[115] The failure of the Soviet Afghan adventure was a large factor in the eventual, peaceful dissolution of that empire. Would Eastern Europe be free today if Afghanistan had never happened? Maybe not. Even knowing the consequences, creating international jihadism may have been the right play.

But how in god's name was it worth giving international Jihadism a shot in the arm to take down Bashar Al-Assad?

Because that's exactly what happened. And it wasn't worth it.

We know about ISIS of course. That's a product of US policy since 2003, but their current power is also a direct result of US policy since 2011. If you read the news carefully, you'll note that much of the power in the supposedly "moderate" regions held by Syrian rebels belongs to the jihadists formerly known as Al Nusra, an Al Queda affiliate. The "moderate" rebels that NATO governments have spent hundreds of millions of dollars to cultivate and support may hold a village or two in northern Syria, but their only real power is located in Washington, DC, Geneva Switzerland and Istanbul, Turkey. The war in Syria has given a PR push and a cause to violent jihadism that it lost with the decline of oil prices in 2008 and the resulting pause in the Iraqi insurgency. The majority of rebel territory is taken and controlled by radical Sunni Islamic Fundamentalists.

There is a very simple way to understand this, that the typical Syria control maps leave out. Syria is divided into 14 governorates. To date the Syrian Opposition has only managed to take four of the least populous provinces. Hassakeh is mostly controlled by the Kurds. ISIS has controlled Raqqa and Deir ez zor since 2013. The opposition's greatest victory came in 2015 when they took the capital city, and most

---

[115] Iran, Iraq, Colombia, El Salvador, Guatemala, Afghanistan, Angola, Sri Lanka, Nicauraga, and I'm sure there were others…

of the province of Idlib. This was done by Jaish Al Fatah, a "moderate opposition" group made up almost exclusively of Al Queda affiliates, and a number of other groups that want to turn Syria into a Sunni Islamic State. It's been clear since 2012, that the only really effective elements in the fight against Assad are radical Sunni fundamentalists.

If Assad falls, that's who the country will end up going to. Jihadists. The US government has known this the whole time. But we have been content to partner with Saudi Arabia against Syria and its partners in Russia and Iran. And this choice has given impetus to terrorist attacks throughout the world.

The "Clash of Civilizations" and the "New 30 Years War"

When you consider the simple truth that "Radical Islamic Terror" is largely a product of US policy, and completely a product of the malicious Saudi state we have protected for half a century, the majority of US commentary goes from looking pointless to looking abjectly amoral. You can go straight to the top of the military industrial complex propaganda machine for examples. Richard N. Haas, the president of the Council on Foreign Relations, has referred to what's going on in the Middle East as the "New Thirty Years War".[116]

In that conflict, religious strife, coupled with the political machinations of 17th century European princes tore Germany to shreds, killing millions. Haas sees this new Thirty Years War as beginning with the Arab Spring in 2011. Interestingly Michael B. Oren, a former Israeli Ambassador to the US, also used this comparison in a book in 2007.[117] The ambassador thought the Middle East's Thirty Years War started with Iranian Revolution in 1979. So, we're on year 38 of a "Thirty Years War" that's projected to last until 2041. Oren was willing to acknowledge the full range of influences, Saudi and American as well as Iranian and Soviet that brought this about. Haas is not.

---

[116] http://www.cfr.org/middle-east-and-north-africa/new-thirty-years-war/p33267

[117] Power, Faith, and Fantasy: America in the Middle East: 1776 to the Present by Michael B. Oren

In a 900+ word summing up of the problems of the region[118], Saudi Arabia is never mentioned by name. Iran is mentioned repeatedly however. That's the state of our "best thinking" on the region. This inability to confront reality opens the door to sillier and more dangerous ideas.

From the day the towers fell, there were elements in the US and Europe who were eager for religious confrontation. These people can be found in the wilder reaches of the internet, but they can be found in our government as well. Michael Flynn, a general who managed to get fired from high positions in both the Obama and Trump administrations, is one example. He has referred to Islam as a cancer.[119] When he's being more polite he refers to "Islamism" as a cancer in the minds of 1.6 Billion Muslims. He sees the issue as a vast "Clash of Civilizations" that could last for decades and goes back over a thousand years.

This is exactly the sort of thing we should be fighting against. It unnecessarily turns a series of easily explained events and influences, laid out in this essay, into a generational war between religions. The danger of such a war actually coming to pass is limited, but we can sacrifice many more lives to its pursuit. The best way to avoid it is to start talking honestly about Saudi Arabia.

SO, WHAT DO WE DO ABOUT SAUDI ARABIA?

Unlike many problems we face, the problem of Saudi Arabia requires little concrete action on our part. What it requires is a change of mentality, and LESS action. Not more.

What's that you say? I've described a tremendously powerful and malign influence that is actively trying to change Islam. Something must be done

---

[118] http://www.cfr.org/middle-east-and-north-africa/new-thirty-years-war/p33267
[119] http://fortune.com/2016/11/19/michael-flynn-criticizes-muslims/

about Saudi Arabia!!! In fact, very little needs to be done. We don't even need to change our formally friendly posture towards Saudi Arabia. We just need to stop preventing their downfall.

Saudi Arabia is toast. Above I described an ever-escalating spiral of radicalization and complexity within the country. At every level of complexity this process was dependent on one thing: rising oil revenues. Saudi Arabia still has its oil. The problem is that the world no longer needs it as badly as it once did. The first Saudi oil embargo in 1973 started off a number of processes that seem to have finally killed Saudi dominance, 40 years later. Proclaiming an era of endless cheap oil is just as foolish as the "peak oil" claims that were pushed with such vigor as recently as three years ago. But it is hard to see how oil prices recover in this decade or the next.

There are just too many downward pressures on price. The energy efficiency revolution that started in the 1970s continues. Our ever-expanding range of consumer goods uses proportionally less energy with every year. The fracking and shale revolutions in the United States and Canada create a natural cap on oil prices. The prospecting oil men have done their job too well. A seemingly endless list of countries have discovered large and exploitable petroleum reserves. In the new low price era, many of these resources can no longer be exploited economically. But many of them can, and the rest lie at the ready should prices rise again. Adoption of electric cars, combined with renewable energy may be oversold, but any serious progress on this front means that much of Saudi Arabia's massive oil reserves are likely to stay in the ground. The era of 100 dollar a barrel oil is over, for the foreseeable future at least.[120]

At some point we will probably start talking about "peak oil" again rather than "peak oil demand", but it will be too late to save the Saudis. Their 28 million people are unaccustomed to working, and have been trained to

---

[120] "The Oil Price And The End Of Islamic Terrorism" More Freedom Foundation. Did I just footnote myself? Why yes, yes I did.

blame any failings on insufficient religiosity. A few years from now, a Saudi king will look to deal with these problems, in the way of Saudi kings, and he will find the larder bare. There will be no money for the people, and there will be no money for the Wahabi religion. On that day the Saudi problem will disappear. It's already disappearing.

OK, So What Do We Not Do?

Saudi Arabia seems to be in the process of solving itself. As this solution evolves, what's important is that we not get in its way. Saudi Arabia has two strategies that it is using to stave off its inevitable fall. Both involve convincing the United States government that they are somehow still a worthwhile partner, despite all the evils they have inspired. They do this by selling the world on two boogie men. They have a lot of support in this propaganda effort from prestige US institutions, both in academia and journalism.

Boogie Man One: IRAN

By fostering the illusion of an imperialist Iran, Saudi Arabia sets itself up as a better option. This is ludicrous. Iran is a fascinating place, with extraordinary potential. It's in bad shape largely because of continued US opposition, not in spite of it. When we stop making it our business to oppose Iran in every context possible, Iran will stop being a problem. The hardline religious regime that they've got going is largely a survival strategy that they've adopted to deal with Saudi-American projects like the Iran-Iraq war, the Axis of Evil, and our attack on Syria, one of Iran's pitifully few allies. Whenever we seriously open up to Iran, the hardline regime falters. If we truly let Iran back into the community of nations, that regime is likely to fade away.

The largest stumbling block here may be a sort of misplaced loyalty. It's true that Saudi Arabia has been an ally of a sort for 70 years. The rivalry between the US and Iran is largely illusory. The rivalry between Saudi Arabia and Iran is not. It's vicious, and it has been going on for 38 years.

We're backing the wrong horse. For 38 years the Iranians have stood up against the most impressive military, economic and diplomatic power the world has ever known. For 38 years the Saudis have had the support of that power, the United States of America, and they are as weak as they've ever been. They've also repaid that support with a massive stab in the back.

Beyond the question of betrayal, there's the hard questions of geopolitics. In an era of declining relative might, can the United States really afford to remain tied to the Saudi Anchor? The Middle East is of less and less importance to us as its dominance of the world oil market fades. Our resources are better used elsewhere. A few decades from now China may present a real threat. If we continue propping up Saudi Arabia, we may be just as mired in the middle east 20 years from now as we are today.

As of this writing, the US government is being drawn more deeply into Saudi Arabia's Yemen quagmire. This is ridiculous. Yemen presents the same complexity as Syria, with the same lack of a plausible "victory". Worse, it even lacks the weak justifications used for the Syrian nightmare. The connections between Iran's Shia theocracy, and the Shia Houthis used to be largely illusory. The groups practice very different forms of Shia Islam. The links are now becoming more real, but that's only because Saudi Arabia started another worthless proxy war in the country. Iran is happy to participate in another Saudi failure. It costs them nothing. Saudi Arabia's actions are creating wider Iranian influence. US participation in this debacle is just dumb.

The other parallel between Syria and Yemen makes it even more important that the United States stays out of it. Both countries feature horrifically indiscriminate bombing of civilian populations. In Syria the villain is Assad, who we oppose. In Yemen the villain is Saudi Arabia, who we arm and support. This path of supporting Saudi Arabia is amoral, foolish, and most importantly no longer viable, in Yemen, or anywhere else. Far better to leave this path before we are forced off of it.

Irritatingly, the Trump administration seems to be continuing along this path. One of the first acts of the newly confirmed CIA head, Mike Pompeo, was to go to Saudi Arabia to confer a medal on a Saudi prince for antiterrorism cooperation.[121] It's now clear that Trump is not going to be delivering the massive shift in Middle East policy that he promised. But many things are moving in the right direction. With Obama's nuclear deal great progress has been made, and despite campaign trail promises, I don't think it's particularly likely that the Trump Administration[122] will bag it completely. So, if we can stay out of Yemen, the de-fanging of the Iran myth may be on the right track. The second issue is not.

Boogie-man Two : Radical Islam

Despite everything documented here, and the evidence of any 5 minute google search on the country, Saudi Arabia has managed to pitch itself as a partner in the fight against "Radical Islam". Incredibly, pretty much everyone in US punditry is willing to play along with this. Miles of columns have been written on the problem of Radical Islam, and very little of it is at all worthwhile. What we all need to do is get more serious about what we're willing to listen to on this topic.

So let's be clear: Anyone who talks about "Radical Islam" without putting Saudi Arabia front and center either has no idea what he is talking about, or he is consciously trying to mislead you.

The broader Islamic "They" do not hate us. Saudi Arabia hates us and has spent hundreds of billions pushing a "clash of civilizations" mentality. The country has spent 50 years trying to crush Islamic diversity. People in US and European media do Saudi Arabia's work for them when they pretend that a religion is to blame for terrorism rather than a very specific ideology, chiefly pushed by one country that is firmly "allied" with the United States. When these writers try to shift the blame from Gulf governments to 1.6 Billion Muslims they aren't just protecting Saudi

[121] http://www.washingtonexaminer.com/trumps-energy-plan-has-him-cozying-up-to-saudi-arabia/article/2614928

[122] I still hate writing that.

Arabia. They are also attempting to shift your attention from the politicians that have aided the Saudi project for decades in Afghanistan and for half a decade now in Syria.

Let's stop listening to fools.

Should you find yourself clicking on another think piece about "Radical Islam", hit ctrl-F and do a quick document search. Is Saudi Arabia mentioned anywhere in the article? If not, then that article is not worth reading.

When Donald Trump first floated his idea of a Muslim ban during his campaign, he stated that it was a temporary measure, just until we "knew what was going on". Well the US government has known exactly what's been going on for quite some time. And now you do too.

For more analysis, and videos on this topic and many others, please join us at...

www.MoreFreedomFoundation.com

A Note on Sources

I'm not usually much of a stickler for footnoting my work. But the story laid out here is controversial enough that I figured it would be wise to cite to some outside authorities. Specifically, I get more serious about citing when I get into the stuff on Saudi Arabia. Three main sources are used for this discussion. They are intentionally drawn from very different ideological backgrounds. Surprisingly, these folks, who might not be able to be sit a room together for very long, are all pretty much in agreement when it comes to Saudi Arabia. I used:

<u>Shadow Wars: The Secret Struggle For the Middle East</u> by Christopher Davidson. Davidson is an academic working in the UK. His work has been favorably cited by the Economist, which is surprising, because he also seems to be more than a bit Marxist. His book is an absolute treasure trove of material, and he is very good at backing up everything he says. I found some of the early material, on European revolution and counter-revolution to be a bit irritating, but his analysis of the post 9/11 and Arab Spring eras is brilliant. That's the left-wing heard from…

<u>Hatred's Kingdom: How Saudi Arabia Supports the New Global Terrorism</u> by Dore Gold, is a bit outdated, but it goes in depth on the central issues of this essay. It's actually a good deal more balanced than that title makes it sound. It dates back to 2003, before Israel and Saudi Arabia started working together as closely as they do now. I doubt it would be published today. Gold was an Israeli ambassador to the United Nations, and he worked for both Benjamin Netanyahu and Ariel Sharon in advisory and diplomatic capacities. I think the analysis of Saudi Arabia is fair and reasoned, though obviously biased whenever Israel comes into the narrative. I suspect that the fire-breathing title comes from the publisher Regnery, which is known as a hyper-conservative house. That's the right-wing heard from…

On Saudi Arabia: It's People, Past, Religion, Fault Lines, and Future By Karen Elliot House. House worked in the Middle east for years for the Wall Street Journal. She was a Middle East correspondent, and the foreign editor. She has won the Pulitzer prize and served as President of Dow Jones International and as publisher of the Wall Street Journal. After retiring she wrote this book on Saudi Arabia, drawing on first-hand experience of the country dating back to the 1970s, and months of new research. Her book manages to both be very sympathetic and convey an incredible sense of frustration. I found this book very useful in softening my rage at the country. Saudi Arabia has abused Islam and the world, but its people are trapped by history as well. And that's the establishment heard from.

Throughout the essay, I cited these books by the last name of the author alone.

46777547R00044

Made in the USA
Lexington, KY
31 July 2019